BATTLE OF THE BULGE

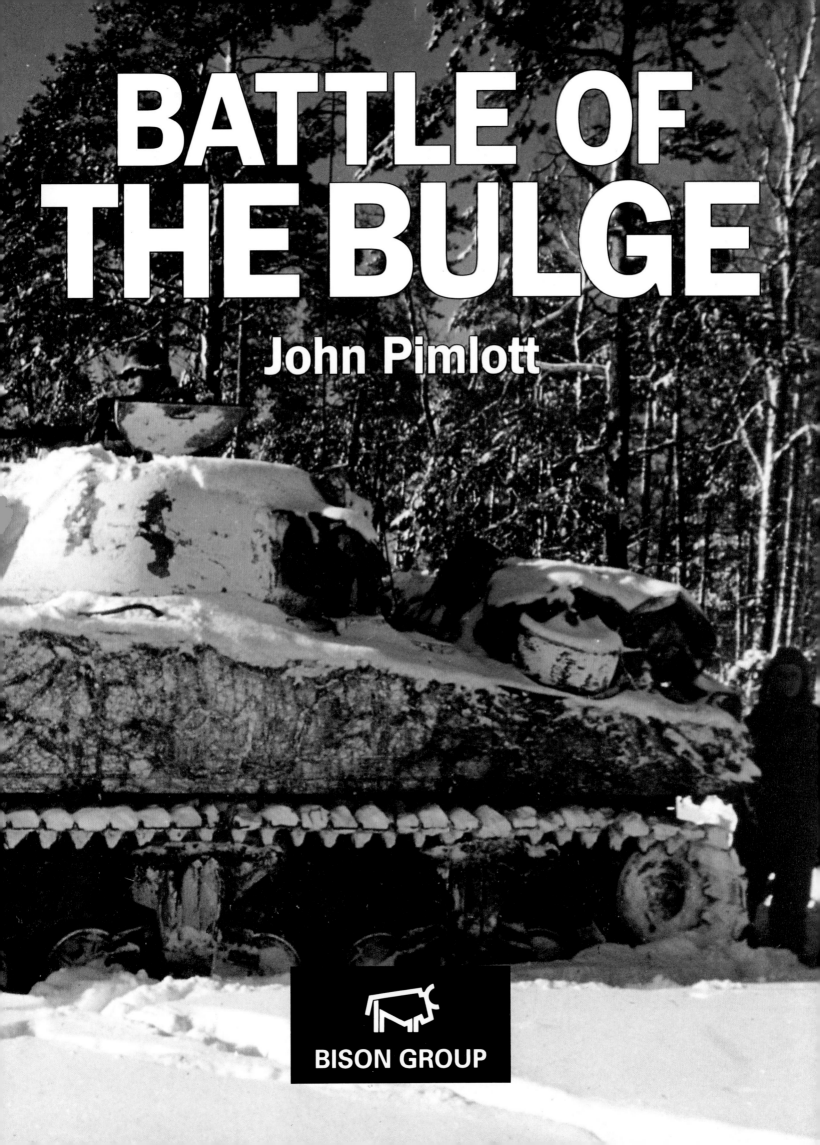

BATTLE OF THE BULGE

John Pimlott

BISON GROUP

First published in 1990
Bison Books Ltd
Kimbolton House
117A Fulham Road
London SW3 6RL

ISBN 0-86124-585-7

Printed in Hong Kong

10 9 8 7 6 5 4 3 2 1

PAGES 2-3: *Sherman tanks prepare
to move off in pursuit of the
retreating German forces in the
final stages of the Battle of the
Bulge.*

PAGE 5: *An armored column of the
US Seventh Army advances
through a village in the Rhône
valley in late August 1944.*

CONTENTS

1
THE ROAD TO
THE ARDENNES

At exactly 0530 hours on Saturday, 16 December 1944, the quiet of the fogenshrouded hills of the Ardennes region in Belgium and Luxembourg was shattered by the crash of a synchronized artillery bombardment. On a front stretching some 85 miles, from Monschau in the north to Echternach in the south, a total of 25 German divisions, 10 of which were armored, stood poised to smash their way through a weak American defensive screen. It was an attempt to repeat the victories of 1940, when German armored formations had advanced with stunning success through exactly the same area. In both cases the aims were the same: to cross the Meuse River, sweep through to the coast and split the Allied armies in two, so causing their collapse.

In 1940 the Allies had been France and Britain, fielding unprepared and antiquated armies which stood little chance against the new, highly mobile technique of Blitzkrieg. Four years later, with amassed experience and more sophisticated weapons, the British had been joined by the Americans, and together they should have been a harder match. However, Allied weakness was epitomized by the fact that the Ardennes was defended by a mere six divisions, with little armored content. The Allies were somewhat complacent about the imminent defeat of Germany. Strategic and tactical surprise was therefore complete on 16 December and the German gamble seemed, for a time, to have been worth the risk. The bitter and confused fighting, under appalling weather conditions, imposed enormous strains on the Allied forces. Although in retrospect it may be seen that eventual Allied victory was never put seriously in doubt, German tanks did penetrate to within a few miles of the Meuse, Anglo-American strategic differences were once more aired in public and, to Hitler and his staff, collapse must have seemed a possibility. After all, it had happened in 1940.

To understand how this situation arose it is necessary to go back six months, to the Allied invasion of Europe. This operation, codenamed Overlord and executed on 6 June, was a risky enterprise. At best the Allied forces, under the supreme command of General Dwight David Eisenhower, could only hope to put five divisions ashore in the first 24 hours. Their method of arrival, over a narrow and congested stretch of sea, was precarious. Support from naval vessels, air fleets and parachute units were vulnerable, and resupply and reinforcement impossible to guarantee. In the event, through a combination of deception, surprise and German hesitation, the assault was successful, although not to the extent envisaged by the Allied planners.

At 0200 hours on 6 June American and British airborne forces dropped on the right and left flanks respectively of the proposed landing area and consolidated temporary positions. Four and a half hours later, after air and naval bombardments, the first wave of ground forces, commanded in the initial phase by General Sir Bernard Montgomery, went ashore on five beaches. Anglo-Canadian units, using specialized armor to overcome defensive obstacles, enjoyed the most success on the Allied left. They managed to link up and advance inland by the end of the day. However, they failed to take one of their main objectives, the important communications center of Caen, and a dangerous gap existed between them and their airborne flank support. The situation was no better on the right. Although American forces had penetrated inland from the westernmost beach (Utah) and made contact with 82nd Airborne Division, they were out on a limb, unconnected to the units on their left which had experienced enormous problems just getting ashore on Omaha beach. By the end of 6 June, the beachhead area was precarious.

PREVIOUS PAGES: *The scene on one of the US invasion beaches in Normandy shortly after the landings of 6 June. Despite often tough opposition, the Allies were able to consolidate their bridgehead and prepare for the breakout into France.*

LEFT: *US troops approach one of the Normandy beaches. The shoreline is littered with damaged and destroyed vehicles, suggesting that these men are part of the second wave of assault troops.*

RIGHT: *US troops wade ashore on Utah, the most westerly of the Allied invasion beaches on D-Day. Encountering little immediate opposition these troops, members of the US VII Corps, made good progress inland and were able to effect a link up with the paratroopers of the US 101st and 82nd Airborne Divisions.*

However, with Hitler firmly convinced that this was merely a feint, designed to draw German units away from the Pas de Calais, counterattacks were piecemeal and a rapid buildup of Allied forces and supplies was allowed to take place. Even so, the envisaged rate of advance soon fell behind schedule and the breakout, essential if success was to be ensured, became a long and painful process of attrition in the close and difficult Normandy countryside. As German reinforcements arrived they were concentrated chiefly around Caen and it was here that some of the hardest fighting took place. By late June it was clear to Montgomery that the Germans were building up their forces, particularly their armor, preparatory to a counterattack against the

RIGHT: *Allied equipment streams ashore during the days following Overlord. Although much severe fighting was taking place at the front, senior Allied commanders were able to plan the exploitation phase of the operation.*

Anglo-Canadian forces. In an attempt to prevent this, he initiated two operations, codenamed Epsom and Goodwood. Epsom, mounted between 26-30 June, was a failure in terms of territory gained as the maximum advance, west of Caen, was only three miles. However, it did cause irreplaceable casualties to the enemy. This process of holding down the German armor continued with Goodwood, initiated on 18 July. Caen itself was at last taken, but the opposition was still considerable. All that the Allies could do was to hold on their left, to the south of Caen, tying down German armor and enabling the Americans on the right to break out, free from solid opposition.

Fortunately by late July the US First Army, under General Omar Bradley, was in a good position. After linking up its beaches on 8 June it pushed westward to sever the Cotentin peninsula, aiming to isolate and capture the port of Cherbourg. This took until 27 June, after which Bradley's army turned south to occupy the base of the peninsula, eventually taking the important town of St Lô on 24 July after hard fighting. It was now poised for the decisive attack, codenamed Cobra. This was launched, after a devastating aerial bombardment, on 25 July. The US VII Corps, under Major General Joseph L Collins, swept forward, reaching Avranches five days later. The stalemate had been broken.

RIGHT: *The brief message sent by General Eisenhower announcing the Allied success on D-Day.*

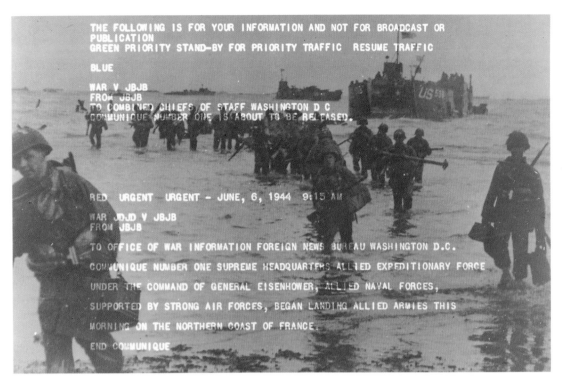

THE FOLLOWING IS FOR YOUR INFORMATION AND NOT FOR BROADCAST OR PUBLICATION
GREEN PRIORITY STAND-BY FOR PRIORITY TRAFFIC RESUME TRAFFIC

BLUE

WAR V JBJB
FROM JBJB
TO COMBINED CHIEFS OF STAFF WASHINGTON D C
COMMUNIQUE NUMBER ONE IS ABOUT TO BE RELEASED.

RED URGENT URGENT - JUNE, 6, 1944 9:15 AM

WAR JBJB V JBJB
FROM JBJB

TO OFFICE OF WAR INFORMATION FOREIGN NEWS BUREAU WASHINGTON D.C.

COMMUNIQUE NUMBER ONE SUPREME HEADQUARTERS ALLIED EXPEDITIONARY FORCE

UNDER THE COMMAND OF GENERAL EISENHOWER, ALLIED NAVAL FORCES,

SUPPORTED BY STRONG AIR FORCES, BEGAN LANDING ALLIED ARMIES THIS

MORNING ON THE NORTHERN COAST OF FRANCE.

END COMMUNIQUE

For the exploitation phase, the Allied forces were re-organized into two army groups; the 12th under Bradley in the west (US First Army under General Courtney H Hodges and Third Army under George S Patton) and the 21st under Montgomery in the east (British Second Army under General Sir Miles Dempsey and Canadian First Army under Henry Crerar). It was Patton's Third Army which led the breakout through the Avranches gap on 1 August, sweeping west into Brittany, south to the Loire and east toward the Seine. At the same time Hodges' First Army and the whole of 21st Army Group attacked southward from the beachhead area, with elements of the former swinging eastward to catch the German divisions facing Caen in the flank. Consequently, as Patton advanced to Orleans, Chartres and Fontainebleau, cutting off German communications to the south, the German Seventh and Fifth Panzer Armies found themselves gradually being squeezed into what became known as the Falaise Pocket. In the event the pocket was not closed completely until 20 August, by which time substantial numbers of men had escaped. However, the Allies did manage to destroy an enormous amount of equipment, chiefly through air attack, and to take some 50,000 prisoners. German defenses west of the Seine collapsed and the way seemed clear for a rapid and decisive Allied advance.

RIGHT: *General Montgomery addresses members of the 50th Division before decorating them for their gallantry on D-Day. The division landed on Gold beach and was primarily involved in the capture of Arromanches and the advance on Bayeux.*

LEFT: *Protected by a high bank, a feature typical of Normandy's bocage, a Sherman tank waits for the order to advance. Although the Sherman was generally outclassed by German armor in 1944, this version, armed with a powerful 17-pounder gun, was at least capable of knocking out heavily armored German tanks at long ranges.*

To begin with, territory was relatively easy to take. Paris was liberated on 25 August, followed by Brussels and Antwerp on 4 September. Indeed, by the end of September most of the hitherto occupied countries of northwest Europe had been cleared of German troops, for in addition to the advances through Belgium and Luxembourg, the US 6th Army Group under General Jacob L Devers had advanced up the Rhône valley from beachheads on the Mediterranean coast (Operation Dragoon) and linked up with Patton's Third Army. Southern and central France therefore fell easily to the Allies and a feeling swiftly arose that the worst was over. As the armies stood ready to close on the next obstacle, the River Rhine, a degree of complacency began to take hold. This was indicated by a private wager between Eisenhower (who had taken personal command of all Allied forces in the field on 3 September) and Montgomery over the duration of hostilities. Eisenhower, flushed with success, bet his subordinate £5 that hostilities would cease by Christmas.

Incidents such as this implied a close relationship between the Allied commanders, but in reality deep divisions were becoming apparent. These were exemplified by a bitter strategic debate which now developed, prin-

LEFT: *A weary member of the 12th SS Panzer Division 'Hitlerjugend' prepares to move out on patrol. This recently raised formation fought a series of bloody engagements against Canadian units during the battle for Caen.*

RIGHT: *Wounded SS troops make their way into captivity during the Allied operations to secure the capture of Caen.*

cipally between Montgomery and Eisenhower, over the method of advance. Montgomery, supported surprisingly by Bradley but opposed vehemently by Patton, favored a deep narrow thrust northward into Holland, designed to cross the Neder Rijn before swinging eastward to isolate the industrial heartland of the Ruhr and racing for Berlin. Eisenhower was aware of problems which his front-line commanders tended to ignore, particularly the problem of supply. Although the important port of Antwerp had been captured the Germans had destroyed much of it before withdrawing and its seaward approaches through the Scheldt estuary were still controlled by the enemy. All supplies still had to be carried from the Normandy lodgment area. As the Allies advanced, this supply line, maintained by a constantly moving convoy of trucks which in fact used more supplies than it delivered, became increasingly tenuous. Eisenhower therefore favored a broad, controlled advance by all the Allied armies together, geared to the supplies available, at least until the area west of the Rhine had been cleared. 21st Army Group found and exploited a weakness in German defenses through Belgium and so received priority of supply (much to Patton's chagrin), but neither Bradley nor Devers was

RIGHT: *The aftermath of an Allied bombing raid – a Panzer IV (left) and a Tiger I of Abteilung 101, a heavy tank battalion assigned to I SS Panzer Corps, lie amid the devastation of Caen.*

expected to hold back. The advance was to be a steady, plodding affair.

Unfortunately, this slowness, combined with the onset of harsher autumn weather, gave the Germans time to recover. In mid-September Montgomery tried to exploit his advantage by using airborne forces to take key bridges in the path of his advance but he was only partially successful. The parachute drops at Eindhoven, Nijmegen and Arnhem (Operation Market) went

in on 17 September and the British Second Army, spearheaded by Lieutenant General Sir Brian Horrocks' XXX Corps, immediately pushed forward to link up (Operation Garden). The bridges at Eindhoven and Nijmegen, taken by men of the US 101st and 82nd Airborne Divisions respectively, were quickly taken. However, German resistance at Arnhem, occupied by the British 1st Airborne Division, proved to be too strong. As the ground forces came to a halt south of the Neder Rijn, the airborne survivors were withdrawn and the northward thrust petered out. Montgomery shifted his emphasis to the Scheldt estuary in the west, intent on clearing Antwerp preparatory to a new drive at the Rhine, the Ruhr and beyond. However, with deteriorating weather and shorter winter days, it was obvious that this could not begin much before the spring.

Between late September and mid-December the situation was similar along much of the Allied line. The exhausted troops, operating at the end of an over-extended supply chain and in steadily worsening conditions, found the going hard. Viewing the front from north to south on the eve of the Ardennes assault, 21st Army Group, with the Canadians on the left and the British on the right, was stuck on the River Maas, with a small salient jutting up to just south of Arnhem. It had achieved only minor advances in the east, toward Venlo and Roermond. Supporting 21st Army Group on its right was the newly-activated US Ninth Army under Lieutenant General William H Simpson – a part of Bradley's enlarged 12th Army Group – which was pressing toward the Roer River against tough opposition. To its right was Hodges' First Army, exhausted after a hard advance against Aachen (taken on 21 October) which had developed into one of the bloodiest battles of the European war, as division after division

ABOVE LEFT: *US paratroopers wait to attack a German strongpoint after friendly artillery fire has prepared the way forward. US forces were tasked with sweeping to the west and south during the exploitation phase of the Overlord operation.*

LEFT: *Infantrymen of the US 331st Infantry Regiment advance through the narrow streets of St Malo. This Brittany port finally fell in the middle of August.*

was decimated in the difficult terrain of the Hurtgen Forest. The losses involved in this battle – 33,000 American casualties in two months – together with the need to mount a fresh offensive against the Roer Dams before the Germans breached them and flooded the countryside, had led to a concentration of forces on Hodges' left. This was one of the reasons why VIII Corps, commanded by Major General Troy Middleton, was spread out so thinly in the Ardennes, an area where action was neither expected nor desired. Only to the south had any deep penetrations been made, with Patton's Third Army advancing through Metz and into the Saar, protecting the left flank of 6th Army Group which had actually reached the Rhine at Strasbourg. Even then, however, a dangerous enemy salient – the Colmar Pocket, containing the German Nineteenth Army – remained in the Vosges mountains. It was an uneven front line, reflecting the inevitable results of Eisenhower's broad advance strategy and, with the majority of forces concentrated in the north and the south, was dangerously weak in the center. It was a weakness which the Germans were ready to exploit.

General Alfred Jodl, Chief of the German Operations Staff, began to study the feasibility of a counteroffensive in the West as early as the first week in September. Under strict instructions from Hitler, whose grip on the strategic direction of German armed forces had become even stronger in the aftermath of the 20 July bomb plot, Jodl concentrated upon certain basic prerequisites. In a special briefing to the Führer, given at OKW (Armed Forces High Command) HQ at Rastenburg in East Prussia on 6 September, he isolated three main problems which would have to be solved: Allied air power, the German supply situation and secrecy of preparation. He went on to postulate that the first could be

negated by mounting the offensive during a period of bad flying weather, the second could be eased by increasing industrial production and a careful allocation of resources, and the third could be solved by restricting information to a select number of relevant planners only, at least in the early stages. Taking all these points into account, he concluded that 1 November would be the earliest possible date for the assault.

The guarded optimism inherent within these findings probably reflected Hitler's known desire for some sort of 'master stroke' in the West, but whether genuinely felt or not, it set the wheels in motion. During the next three weeks Hitler and Jodl analyzed the Allied advance, trying to discern its strategic shape and find an area of potential weakness. By mid-September, as a definite front line began to emerge, they concluded:

ABOVE RIGHT: *The remains of a German convoy, testament to the power and efficiency of Allied ground-attack aircraft, lie by the side of a French road. The closure of the Falaise Gap in late August, in part effected by Allied air power, led to the capture of thousands of irreplaceable German troops and the destruction of much equipment.*

RIGHT: *Jubilant Parisians greet the arrival of US forces. The French capital, although relatively untouched by the war, saw bitter fighting between the German garrison and civilians before it was liberated on 25 August.*

Eifel to the east was ideal for a secret concentration of attack formations.

Five days later selected members of Jodl's staff were given their first indication of the plan when Hitler, in a monologue reminiscent of the heady days of 1940, painted a picture of extraordinary detail to them. He began by outlining the broad concept of the offensive – a breakthrough on the Ardennes front which would enable armored units to cross the Meuse between Liège and Namur preparatory to a rapid advance on Antwerp which would split the Allied armies in two and lead to their collapse. He went on to discuss in some depth how this was to be achieved. He estimated that a minimum of 30 divisions would be needed, 10 of which would have to be armored. These would be organized into four armies. Those on the north and south of the assault area – around Monschau and Echternach respectively – would be composed almost entirely of infantry, with the task of pressing forward to protect the main assault from flank attack. For the main assault, two Panzer armies, containing a mixture of tank and infantry formations, would be used. After a short sharp artillery bombardment designed to confuse the defenders, infantry units would advance on a 50-mile front to isolate or take out the forward American positions. This would open the way for the armor which would, in the Blitzkrieg pattern of 1940, find and exploit lines of least resistance, by-passing defensive locations and leaving them to be mopped up by the following infantry. The aim at all times was to be Antwerp, with no deviations whatsoever. The tanks were to force the Meuse on the second day, swing northeastward around Brussels and reach the coast before the Allied High Command could react. If the old magic could be regained, the Allied front would crack wide open and, after an initial period of shock, would quickly degenerate into panic and col-

that the Allies lacked a strategic reserve capable of being used to plug any gap made by a counteroffensive; that Anglo-American cooperation was little more than a veneer, implying that Allied reaction to a German attack would be slow and disjointed; and that the Allied center was thinly held. The last mentioned discovery suited Hitler's strategic instinct. By 20 September he was convinced that the Ardennes was the key to success, as it had been in 1940, not only because of the scarcity of Allied forces in the area but also because the heavily-wooded, almost mountainous country of the

ABOVE LEFT: *The people of Brussels crowd around a camouflage-bedecked Cromwell tank of the Guards Armored Division, 3 September 1944.*

LEFT: *While the Allies were making excellent progress in the drive through northern Europe in the late summer of 1944, other forces were beginning the liberation of southern France. The operation, codenamed Dragoon, began with landings to the east of Marseilles on 15 August and made steady progress. Here, German troops surrender to US infantrymen in a coastal town to the west of Toulon.*

RIGHT: *The opening stages of Operation Dragoon in southern France. French and US forces faced second-grade German formations and, although occasional pockets of tough resistance had to be neutralized, the advance went smoothly.*

lapse. At this point, according to Hitler, the Anglo-American alliance would fall apart, the war-weary British would surrender and the demoralized Americans would withdraw to concentrate on their war in the Pacific. With the West thus secure, all German forces could turn against the menace from the East, saving European culture from the Bolshevik hordes and, like the Prussian hero Frederick the Great in 1762, snatch victory from the jaws of defeat. It was an ambitious, almost insane, plan, but Hitler's charisma was still strong enough to fire the enthusiasm of his close

advisers. He called for a draft operation plan to be drawn up immediately, based on a projected date of attack in late November.

In retrospect, it may be seen that the entire concept contained within it the seeds of its own destruction. From the outset the idea of a counteroffensive, the choice of ground, the allocation of forces, the tactics and timings all emanated from Hitler alone and owed more to his strategic 'insight' than to any deep General Staff analysis of the true situation. This was guaranteed to cause problems with the professional army officers in-

RIGHT: *Men of the British 1st Airborne Division prepare to advance from their landing site to Arnhem. The operation, known as Market Garden, was an attempt to cut through to the German industrial center of the Ruhr. The operation failed to achieve all of its objectives, forcing the Allies to prepare for another year of war.*

LEFT: *Dutch civilians celebrate the liberation of Eindhoven. Although the Allied forces had made good progress after the push from Normandy, their supply lines were becoming severely overextended.*

RIGHT: *The objectives of the German offensive in the Ardennes. By slicing through the relatively undefended region, the Germans hoped to reach the Belgian port of Antwerp, thereby splitting the Allied armies. Given the resources available to the Germans, the difficult terrain and the worsening weather, the operation was by any standards extremely ambitious.*

BELOW LEFT: *General George Patton, one of the more charismatic Allied commanders, was destined to play a key role in the eventual defeat of the German thrust.*

BELOW RIGHT: *By late 1944 Adolf Hitler was facing defeat. Gambling all on a decisive victory in the West, he stripped the equally vulnerable Eastern Front of many irreplaceable divisions to boost the forces available for the Ardennes attack.*

volved in the attack, for not only were they not consulted in the initial planning stage but they were also to be allowed little initiative or freedom of maneuver once the attack began. The plan was too rigid, reflecting perhaps the development of Blitzkrieg over the previous four years. In 1940 the technique had been one of flexibility and improvisation but by 1944 it had become a 'theory,' with preconceptions about its effectiveness.

Thus for Hitler to call for speed and no deviation from the main objective was restrictive and, given the geography of the Ardennes, shortsighted. His choice of area for the attack may be understandable, but his presumption that big, heavy tanks could advance quickly and easily through forests and hills, down steep-sided narrow roads and across a myriad of streams and rivers in atrocious winter conditions was leaving too much to chance. A determined defense of key crossroads, junctions or communication centers, or the destruction of selected bridges, could wreck the careful timings of the initial advance completely.

These were all 'intangibles,' glossed over in the euphoria engendered by Hitler's enthusiasm, and in late September OKW staff officers had other, more immediate concerns. Chief among these was the collection and organization of the forces required for the assault. As early as 25 September Field Marshal Gerd von Rundstedt, Commander in Chief, West, was ordered to withdraw I and II SS Panzer Corps from the front line, ostensibly for rest and reorganization. In reality, however, they were to constitute the backbone of a newly activated SS Panzer Army – the Sixth, under the trusted Nazi SS Oberstgruppenführer Josef 'Sepp' Dietrich – which was to form the main assault force on the German right, responsible for the thrust between Monschau and St Vith. Its infantry component, together with the bulk of those for the other three armies, was to be provided from the *Volksgrenadier* Divisions currently being put together in Germany from among the latest batch of conscripts, men from broken formations and even personnel from disbanded air force and naval units. It was estimated that 10 of these divisions could be made available by 20 November, a further three by 30 November and a total of 20 by 10 December. They would be joined by the more conventional infantry divisions already holding the Ardennes sector, under Fifteenth Army in the north and Seventh Army in the south. The second of the assault tank formations, responsible for the sector between St Vith and Wiltz, was to be Fifth Panzer Army, commanded by General Hasso von Manteuffel, currently fighting in the south but to be withdrawn for reorganization in late October. All units would be part of Army Group B, under Field Marshal Walther Model, theoretically subject to orders from Rundstedt but, for the purposes of the attack, answerable directly to Hitler at OKW. All this was agreed to at another of Jodl's briefings, on 11 October, and a code name for the plan – *Wacht am Rhein* – was assigned.

Secrecy was still a major consideration. OKW announced to all commanders on the Western Front that it was not possible to stage a counteroffensive in the foreseeable future. However, as the plans became more specific the circle of those in the know had to be widened. On 21 October Hitler personally briefed SS Obersturmbannführer Otto Skorzeny, a renowned commando leader, on the part he was to play. He was ordered to recruit English-speaking soldiers from throughout the armed forces, organize them into the so-called 150th Panzer Brigade and, in an operation code named *Greif*, infiltrate them through the American lines, in American uniforms, to create maximum disruption in rear areas as the main assault went in. It was a minor part of the overall plan, but one which was to enjoy considerable success.

The following day, 22 October, was devoted to briefing Generals Siegfried Westphal and Hans Krebs, chiefs of staff to Rundstedt and Model respectively, and here the problems began. Neither officer was impressed with the broad sweep of the *Wacht am Rhein* concept, fearing not only that it was too optimistic but also that too little time had been allowed for its preparation.

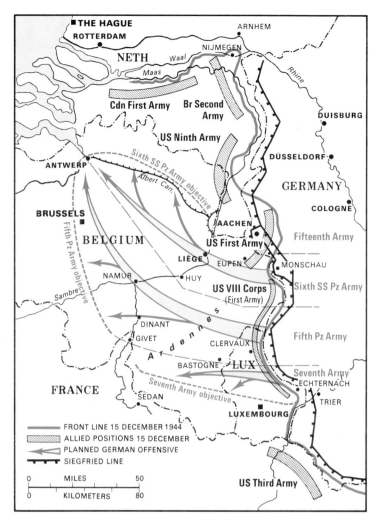

They went back to their superiors full of doubts and questions, and these were reflected in papers submitted to Hitler by both Rundstedt and Model in late October, offering scaled-down alternatives. Rundstedt favored a breakthrough just to the Meuse with the aim of trapping the Allied divisions facing the Siegfried Line. Model suggested a pincer attack, to be carried out by Fifth Panzer Army from the Ardennes and Fifteenth Army from Aachen, again with the aim of trapping American front-line formations rather than winning the war at a stroke. Such reservations were inevitable from men who had been fighting for over five years, who had seen defeat and had come to distrust Hitler's 'grand slam' strategic solutions. Their views were anathema to the Führer, by now convinced that all professional army officers were defeatists and plotters. Two concessions were made, caused more by the Allied attacks against Fifteenth Army around Aachen and the Hurtgen Forest than by the misgivings of the field commanders. Fifteenth Army, fighting for its existence, was deleted from the *Wacht am Rhein* plan and the assault date was postponed, initially to 10 December and finally to 16 December. Neither date satisfied the field marshals. As late as 2 December, in a special meeting in Berlin, Model, ably supported by Manteuffel, tried desperately to persuade Hitler to accept his 'little slam' alternative, but to no avail. Rundstedt, virtually squeezed out of the command chain by this time, disassociated himself from the whole affair. The die was cast, but those responsible for the plan's execution had strong reservations.

Final orders were issued on 11 December and three days later the attack formations moved quietly up to the front line from their concentration areas in the Eifel. Their arrival boosted the strength of the Ardennes sector to 23 divisions, with a further two in reserve, and of this total 10 were armored. Running

from north to south, Dietrich had under his command four Panzer Divisions (1st SS, 2nd SS, 9th SS and 12th SS), one Parachute Division (3rd, in an infantry role) and four *Volksgrenadier* Divisions (12th, 246th, 277th and 326th). He fielded a total of 450 tanks and self-propelled guns. To his left, Manteuffel also had nine divisions, but fewer AFVs (about 350), for although he commanded four Panzer Divisions (2nd, 9th, Panzer *Lehr* and 116th) as well as the 15th Panzer Grenadier Division, none was up to full strength. They varied between 60-80 percent effective. They were supported by the 18th, 26th, 62nd and 560th *Volksgrenadier* Divisions. To Manteuffel's left, in the deep south of the assault area, Seventh Army under General Erich Brandenberger contributed five divisions (5th Parachute, 79th Infantry, 212th, 276th and 352nd *Volksgrenadier*), but had no armor at all. OKW held a reserve of two full-strength divisions (3rd Panzer Grenadier and 9th *Volksgrenadier*) and two elite brigades (*Führer Begleit* and *Führer Grenadier*), to be released on the express orders of Hitler alone. Taken overall, this was less than Jodl had originally promised, but with 275,000 men, 1900 heavy artillery pieces and 950 AFVs available, a formidable force had been gathered together.

Facing this force in mid-December were six American divisions, totaling little more than 75,000 men, and theoretically in no condition to withstand an assault. In the north, opposite Dietrich's right, were the 2nd and 99th Infantry Divisions, part of Major General Leonard Gerow's V Corps. The 99th had been in the line about a month and was not battle hardened; indeed the 2nd was in the process of attacking *through* them as part of the advance toward the Roer Dams. Even the veteran status of the 2nd – it had been in the thick of the fighting since Normandy – was of little immediate value because of this complex maneuver, while its concentration for the assault had left a defensive gap to the south. This region, stretching for two miles in the area of the strategically important Losheim gap, was osten-

ABOVE LEFT: *German infantrymen advance across a shell-blasted street in Arnhem during the final days of the battle.*

LEFT: *German grenadiers prepare to move into action supported by a pair of Panther tanks, September 1944.*

RIGHT: *British paratroopers man a shell hole on the outskirt of Arnhem. The 1st Airborne Division virtually ceased to exist after its heroic defense of the aptly named 'Bridge too Far.'*

BELOW: *Wary of drawing fire from German snipers, US troops prepare to advance down a street in Aachen. The fighting for this city and the nearby Hurtgen Forest was both bitter and prolonged.*

sibly covered by 14th Cavalry Group – a portion of 2nd Division not needed in the Roer Dams attack – but it was overstretched and poorly deployed. It was also still under command of Middleton's VIII Corps (whence 2nd Division had recently come) in an arrangement guaranteed to cause chaos and confusion. It held the corps interface, responsible for tying together Gerow's force and those of Middleton and was neither briefed nor deployed to carry out its task. It was a dangerous gap in an area earmarked by Dietrich for his armored advance.

The northernmost of Middleton's units was the newly arrived 106th Infantry Division, recently moved into what was known as the Schnee Eifel region to replace 2nd Division. Its area of responsibility was in fact a part of Germany, jutting out in a salient of small villages, hills and steepsided valleys which begged to be bitten off – a process high on the list of priorities facing troops of Manteuffel's right wing. Major General Alan Jones, commanding the 106th, considered his position to be exposed and overextended, opinions shared by Major General Norman D 'Dutch' Cota, commanding the veteran 28th Infantry Division to his south. The 28th, sent to the Ardennes to recover from horrific casualties suffered in the Hurtgen Forest, was responsible for 23 miles of front, facing the Our River, a fast-flowing waterway which the bulk of Manteuffel's armor had to cross. An adequate defense was little short of impossible. To the right of the 28th was part of another new division, 9th Armored (later to achieve fame as the captor of the intact Remagen bridge over the Rhine in March 1945), which, although responsible for only six miles of front, was overstretched since two of its three combat command were being held back as Middleton's mobile reserve. They faced attacks from Brandenberger's forces, although the bulk of these were arrayed against the last of the US divisions in the line, the 4th Infantry, another veteran division recovering from the Hurtgen Forest battle. All in all, American defenses were in poor condition. Lulled into a false sense of security by the quiet of the Ardennes sector, taken in by German deceptions and secrecy, and composed of a dangerous mixture of combat-weary and 'green' troops, the units were about to face an absolutely overwhelming assault.

2
OPERATION
WACHT AM RHEIN

The initial artillery bombardment, in the predawn dark and cold of 16 December, lasted approximately three-quarters of an hour. Its aim appears not to have been the destruction of front-line American units – because of the need for secrecy and the lack of time available, few German commanders had plotted such locations accurately – but the severing of communications as a preliminary move in the policy of creating confusion. In this, the artillery succeeded. All along the front line small American outposts – the sharp end of divisional deployments – suddenly found themselves isolated from higher command elements, a state of affairs which left them unsure about what to do and confused about what was happening. The first day of the battle is therefore extremely difficult to describe in generalized terms for it quickly and inevitably dissolved into a series of small-unit actions. Furthermore, as each of these small units, unaware of what was going on to its right or left, imagined that it alone was being attacked, the overall picture which gradually seeped through to divisional, army and army group commanders was fragmentary and impossible to analyze. The chaos which Hitler saw as a vital prerequisite to success was therefore well-advanced by the end of the first 24 hours. The shape of the future battle could also be discerned. The German assault divisions could not break through and destroy American defenses with ease. A significant number of small units, in a remarkable display of initiative and stubbornness, stood firm, holding the enemy advance for vital hours or even days. As the Germans should have learned from their experience on the Eastern Front, Blitzkrieg could be countered by defense in depth. In many cases, without realizing it, the small units in action on 16 December were helping to form such a defense and contributing significantly to the eventual failure of *Wacht am Rhein.*

This may be seen to good effect in the north, where Dietrich planned to push aside the 99th Division, take the important Elsenborn Ridge and break through the Losheim gap. For the frontal assault he deployed three divisions, 3rd Panzer Grenadier, 12th and 277th *Volksgrenadier*, on his right against the main American locations and 3rd Parachute on his left to open up the Losheim gap. In addition he had ordered Colonel Friedrich-August von der Heydte to organize a parachute landing into the Baraque Michel mountain area, a few miles north of Malmédy, with the aim of securing the important road junction at Baraque Michel through which the armored spearheads of 12th SS Panzer Division would move in their advance on Liège. It was classic Blitzkrieg, reminiscent of the attacks on Holland and Belgium in 1940, but it did not go smoothly. As early as 0400 hours on 16 December von der Heydte, impatiently awaiting the arrival of nearly half his force at Lippspringe airfield, was forced to postpone the operation as trucks to carry the men from their billets had not turned up.

Reponsibility for the northern breakthrough therefore rested with the ground forces alone and, in the first 24 hours, results were mixed. The attack upon 99th Division began well enough, with infantry and assault pioneer units moving deep into American lines under cover of fog and howling winds, but the expected collapse did not materialize. Under the impression that this was merely a spoiling attack, designed to upset the advance on the Roer Dams, and steadied significantly by the presence of the battle-hardened 2nd Division, the greenhorns of the 99th acquitted themselves well. An attack upon Buchholz Station in the south, near the corps divide, was beaten off by noon; heavy fighting in the twin towns of Rocherath and Krinkelt in the center did not produce an American withdrawal; and the area

PAGES 22-23: *Apprehensive US prisoners trudge into captivity as a Tiger II continues to advance westward. Caught off guard, the overstretched Allied forces in the Ardennes were forced into retreat during the first stages of Operation* Wacht am Rhein.

RIGHT: *A heavily camouflaged StuG III assault gun moves into action. The German buildup of forces in the Ardennes was extremely meticulous and the Allies had little inkling of the assault.*

of Monschau-Höfen in the far north was successfully defended. Indeed, by the end of the day the bulk of 99th Division had not been shifted from its original positions. Hodges, unaware of the true nature of the German offensive, had refused permission to cancel 2nd Division's attack toward the northeast.

Not all of the 99th survived the day. One platoon, stationed at the road junction of Lanzerath, had borne the full weight of 3rd Parachute Division and, not surprisingly, succumbed. It did succeed in delaying the German advance until dusk, however, regardless of the fact that its neighboring unit in the Losheim gap, a squadron of 14th Cavalry Group at Manderfeld, had withdrawn southward during the morning after heavy fighting. In fact 14th Cavalry was all but destroyed, losing most of its equipment and seeing many of its subunits surrounded, annihilated or dispersed, and this opened the Losheim gap completely. Even so, 3rd Parachute Division had suffered heavy casualties and had been forced to divert valuable resources to take out isolated

LEFT: *A Panther tank moves through the Ardennes. Thick forest and cloudy weather helped to conceal the German preparations from the Allies.*

RIGHT: *Clad against near-freezing temperatures, German infantry examine the remains of US transport vehicles abandoned during the first hours of the onslaught. US supplies of food, ammunition and clothing were much sought after.*

bridging equipment with which to cross the Our, a massive traffic jam had quickly built up on the east bank of the river. Sixth SS Panzer Army, far from racing easily to the Meuse, was getting dangerously bogged down.

By comparison, Fifth Panzer Army achieved far more, partly because Manteuffel's area of attack included easier ground and partly because of the weaknesses in the strength and deployment of the American divisions facing him. He had three major aims. On his left, south of Dasburg, General Heinrich Freiherr von Lüttwitz's XLVII Panzer Corps, comprising three divisions (2nd Panzer, Panzer *Lehr* and 26th *Volksgrenadier*) was to cross the Ourthe River, seize Clervaux (Clerf) and the important road junction at Bastogne, and cross the Meuse south of Namur. Farther north, General Walter Krüger's LVIII Panzer Corps, containing two divisions (116th Panzer and 560th *Volksgrenadier*) was to cross the Our near Lutzkampen, take the town of Houffalize, skirt the Ourthe River to its right and cross the Meuse between Namur and Andenne. Finally, in almost a subsidiary action on the extreme right, elements of General Walter Lucht's LXVI Infantry Corps were to nip out the Schnee Eifel salient preparatory to capturing St Vith and protecting the northern flank of Fifth Panzer Army. Thus the entire assault was concentrated against 28th and 106th US Infantry Divisions, strung out in a series of isolated and vulnerable outposts and unprepared for battle. The outcome was inevitable.

The 106th Division, concentrated in the Schnee Eifel, was in trouble even before Lucht's attack, spearheaded by 18th *Volksgrenadier*, began. Once 14th Cavalry Group to their north withdrew under heavy pressure, the Losheim gap opened up, enabling German troops to infiltrate to the rear. These troops spend much of the day locating and attacking artillery units, forcing them

American outposts. Dietrich had been obliged to commit 12th SS Panzer earlier than intended in an effort to maintain momentum and this had caused further problems. With deep snow obscuring the roads and a lack of

ABOVE LEFT: *Apprehensive US prisoners march into detention under the watchful eye of two SS officers. The prisoners had good reason to be wary as the SS showed little concern for many prisoners, as latter events in the Ardennes were to show.*

ABOVE RIGHT: *The other side of the coin. The offensive, at least temporarily, liberated several German towns. Here local inhabitants of one such settlement greet German assault troops.*

LEFT: *Bewildered US troops, caught out by the ferocity of the initial German advance, prepare to move out to a new defensive position somewhere to the rear of the original front. Some units disintegrated, some cracked, others fought with great skill and determination.*

RIGHT: *A still from a German propaganda film made at the time of the offensive showing infantrymen advancing past a wrecked US mechanized unit.*

to withdraw and effectively cutting off the three regiments of the 106th from their fire support. Thus, although German frontal assaults were held at Bleialf in the center and Winterspelt in the south, a deep penetration had been made in the north, in the Losheim gap, and the 106th was effectively isolated. In the absence of clear information, Major General Jones, in his headquarters at St Vith, was paralyzed, although becoming acutely aware that the entire Schnee Eifel region, containing the bulk of his division, was in very great danger of being taken out. He was perhaps fortunate not to realize that virtually nothing now stood between himself and the northern arm of the 18th *Volksgrenadier* assault.

Nor was this the only German breakthrough in Manteuffel's sector, for the main emphasis of his assault, delivered by XLVII and LVIII Panzer Corps, was concentrated against 28th Division, with predictable results. Major General Cota had deployed his three front-line regiments as best he could, with the 112th in the north, linking with the right of 106th Division, the 110th in the center and the 109th in the south, bordering 9th Armored Division lines. In the event, the two flank regiments held firm during 16 December – the 112th denied two important bridges across the Our to 116th Panzer while the 109th held up an attack by three German infantry battalions – but the center cracked wide open. The 110th Regiment, only recently taken over by Colonel Hurley Fuller, a veteran of the Argonne Forest in World War I, was overstretched even by the generous terms of the time and was strung out in a number of isolated posts on what was known as 'Skyline Drive,' an exposed supply route running parallel to the front. These posts were hit by the infantry units of XLVII Panzer Corps, which quickly infiltrated through the defensive gaps in their advance to Clervaux. Despite

Hitler's orders, however, they could not afford to leave the American positions intact in their rear and, in a series of closequarter engagements in deep snow, the 110th Regiment inflicted heavy losses and did not col-

LEFT: *German assault troops smile for the camera against the backdrop of a wrecked truck. The momentum of their initial assault was not to last, however.*

RIGHT: *SS troops discuss the tactical situation while a handful of dazed prisoners await their fate. One SS man carries a Panzerfaust 60 antitank projectile over his shoulder.*

BELOW LEFT: *German troops move down the side of a country road in the Ardennes.*

BELOW RIGHT: *US troops dig in along the edge of a wood. One of their comrades, probably the victim of sniper fire, lies in the foreground. Many US formations, although relatively 'green' or understrength, worked hard to take the edge off the German offensive.*

lapse immediately. Hand-to-hand battles and costly sieges in villages such as Weiler, Holzthum, Munshausen and Marnach slowed down the German advance significantly. They could not stop it entirely. As Lüttwitz threw bridges across the Our at Gemund and Dasburg, pushing the first of his heavy tanks to the western bank soon after nightfall, the road to Clervaux and Bastogne lay open. The 110th Regiment, isolated and gradually succumbing to the pressure, virtually ceased to exist.

Meanwhile, farther south, Brandenberger's Seventh Army, charged with the twin tasks of breaking through to protect Manteuffel's left flank and of demonstrating toward Luxembourg in an effort to tie down American reserves, had followed a pattern which Dietrich would have found familiar. Two divisions, 5th Parachute and 352nd *Volksgrenadier* of the LXXXV Infantry Corps, attacked on his right but the forward elements encountered difficult terrain and were held by the US 109th Regiment. According to the commander of the 109th, the regiment 'did not even consider giving up any ground,' a remarkable statement given the overwhelming odds and one which was to mean little once Colonel Fuller's regiment to the immediate north had collapsed late in the day. In Brandenberger's center a similar lack of headway ensued as the Combat Command of the 9th Armored, holding a narrow sector and enjoying the support of an entire field artillery battalion, inflicted heavy casualties on the 276th *Volksgrenadier* Division of LXXX Infantry Corps. Things went slightly better in the extreme south, where the 12th Infantry Regiment of 4th Division bore the brunt of an assault across the Sauer River by the 212th *Volksgrenadiers*, for predawn infiltrations, coupled with overwhelming numbers, led to forward outposts being surrounded and besieged in a series of small villages. The 12th Regiment was the only element of 4th Division to be attacked and the divisional commander, Major General Raymond O Barton, was able to build up a strong reserve, including armor, and prepare it for commitment. The southern shoulder

of the Ardennes had therefore not been broken, and although heavy fighting was still to take place, leading eventually to a breakthrough by 5th Parachute Division, Seventh Army as a whole was to make little further progress.

Thus, by the end of 16 December, German gains were quite small. Very little had been achieved on either of the two flanks and Dietrich's army, upon which the main onus for the advance to the Meuse rested, had not made the expected breakthrough. In the center, elements of 28th Division seemed to be holding on. This was a superficial view. In both north and south important bridges had been captured or constructed, the Losheim gap and Skyline Drive were breached and, despite the traffic jams developing behind Dietrich's sector, the armor was about to be committed. As in so many modern battles, the first day had been one of probing, finding and opening lines of least resistance, ready for more dramatic advances thereafter. In short, the German forces were poised for breakthrough.

Even so, it would be wrong to see 16 December as a German victory. The American forces, even those completely new to battle, had not collapsed as soon as pressure was exerted upon them and in nearly all sectors had inflicted irreplaceable casualties, slowing the Germans down and delaying their advance. More significantly, the Allied High Command did not split or fail to react. Regardless of Hitler's beliefs, Eisenhower was making redeployments to answer the threat within the first 24 hours. News of the assault finally reached his HQ in Paris after dusk on 16 December. The Supreme Commander, aided by Bradley who happened to be visiting, ordered two armored divisions – the 7th in Ninth Army sector and the 10th with Patton in the

south – to be withdrawn from the line and sent to the Ardennes. A few hours later XVIII Airborne Corps, under Major General Matthew B Ridgway, was directed to send its two European-based divisions, 82nd and 101st Airborne, to Bastogne. The strategic reserve which OKW had calculated did not exist had been created and committed in a very short time. It was an indication of Allied flexibility which the Germans had failed to recognize.

The importance of the initial American resistance to the attack may be seen throughout the ensuing battle, for although German armor was able to push forward in three key sectors – in the north to the Amblève River and around St Vith, and in the south around Bastogne – carefully laid down timings had been disrupted, in some cases decisively. As the battle progressed and American resistance hardened into more organized defensive lines, the crossing of the Meuse – which was only the *first* objective – gradually became less and less feasible. Nowhere was this more apparent than in the north, where Dietrich's Sixth Panzer Army found itself slowly but effectively hemmed in and denied the massive breakthrough it so desperately needed.

The first major setback took place in the far north of Dietrich's assault sector, in the area covered by the US 2nd and 99th Divisions. By the end of the first day they had managed to hold firm but were dangerously vulnerable, particularly as Hodges was insisting upon a continuation of the attack toward the Roer Dams. No military formation, however flexible, can be expected to attack and defend simultaneously and, fortunately, this was recognized at 0730 hours on 17 December. Hodges authorized General Gerow to defend his corps front as he saw fit, an order which Gerow thankfully took to mean that 2nd Division's attack could be canceled. This changed the entire situation in the north, especially when Gerow delegated responsibility for defense to Major General Walter M Robertson, the experienced commander of 2nd Division. Robertson immediately reviewed the overall situation, recognized the confusion caused by the previous day's battle and ordered a withdrawal of both divisions to the strategically important Elsenborn Ridge, two miles to the rear. Here they would be joined by one of the most experienced formations in the European theater – 1st

RIGHT: *The remains of a Jagdpanther self-propelled antitank gun. Although it was produced in comparatively small numbers, this tank-destroyer was a potent weapon, capable of dealing with Allied armor at long ranges.*

BELOW: *The various stages of Operation* Wacht am Rhein. *The German forces in the vicinity of Bastogne made the greatest progress but nevertheless failed to secure their initial objectives. To the north and south, the extent of the advance was much less due to the solidity of the US defenses.*

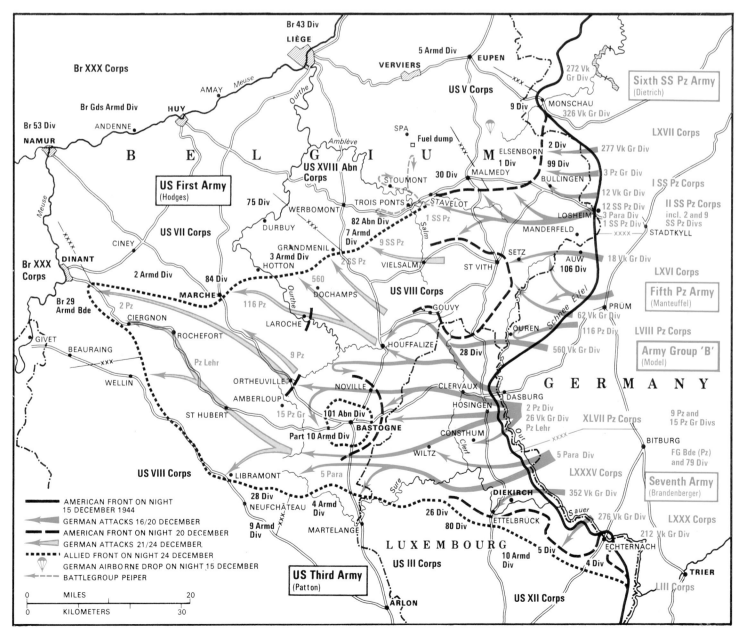

Infantry Division, released by Gerow from reserve.

Robertson faced a daunting and extremely difficult task. The withdrawal of units from the thick of a battle is fraught with danger, particularly if some of those units are new to combat. In addition, by 17 December the whole area was hopelessly confused. In the face of continuing German attacks, 2nd and 99th Divisions had become intermingled, fighting was taking place all over the area, command networks were overstretched and the roads were packed with equipment, while to the south the Losheim gap had been forced, exposing

Robertson's flank. Displaying remarkable coolness, the new commander worked out and implemented a plan. His first priority was to recover those elements of 2nd Division concentrated in the northeast for the Roer Dams attack, and for this reason 99th Division was ordered to hold on to its current positions as a protective screen. This complex maneuver was completed during 17 December, with 2nd Division moving into Rocherath and Krinkelt, important locations as they controlled the roads leading up to the Elsenborn Ridge from the east. Once in position, the 2nd acted as a blocking force

ABOVE: *Members of the US 1st Infantry Division's 26th Regiment move forward to repel the German advance at Butgenbach, a village some 15 miles northeast of St Vith on the Elsenborn Ridge.*

LEFT: *The execution of one of Otto Skorzeny's Greif commandos. Wearing captured US combat fatigues and civilian clothing, they were supposed to sow confusion behind US lines. For the most part their efforts ended in failure.*

through which the remnants of 99th Division could withdraw. This was a dangerous move, for throughout 17-18 December the three front-line regiments of the 99th were under sustained attack from 12th SS Panzer, and 12th and 277th *Volksgrenadier* Divisions, and were being directed to disengage under fire. It was thus extremely fortuitous that Dietrich, frustrated by lack of progress in the north, chose just this moment to redeploy 12th SS Panzer, moving it from opposite Rocherath to help in the exploitation through the Losheim gap. The pressure was taken off 99th Division sufficiently to enable it to make a fighting withdrawal, through Rocherath-Krinkelt to the Elsenborn positions, late on 18 December. The 2nd Division followed on 19 December and, once up on the ridge, these units set up a solid defense line. They were joined by 1st Division and elements of 9th Division which had moved down from north of Monschau. This force successfully withstood repeated German infantry attacks. Casualties were heavy (99th Division alone lost 2200 men between 16-20 December) but a barrier had been created on the northern shoulder. It was a major contribution to eventual American victory.

Dietrich had no more luck with the 'specialist' force attached to his command, for although both von der Heydte and Skorzeny committed their units during this early phase, neither achieved its allotted task. As early as 0300 hours on 17 December von der Heydte's parachute drop into the Baraque Michel area, postponed the day before, met with complete disaster. In atrocious weather conditions, which included ground winds of up to 50 feet per second, and plagued by problems caused by lack of recent jumping experience, the force was distributed far and wide, some of the men actually landing as far afield as Bonn. Von der Heydte himself found the dropping zone but, with less than 130 of his soldiers joining him by the end of the day, there was little he could do. He and his men went to ground, avoiding con-

tact with American units, and finally surrendered on 22 December. At the same time, selected groups of Skorzeny's *Greif* commandos, dressed in American uniforms, infiltrated behind enemy lines, where they cut telephone wires, misdirected traffic and even reached the Meuse, but in the absence of a supporting advance all were soon captured, killed or withdrawn. Many of those captured were in fact shot by the Americans as spies, an inevitable consequence of their deception.

In purely military terms, none of these 'specialists' achieved a great deal and their use can be dismissed as

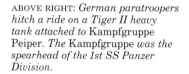

ABOVE RIGHT: *German paratroopers hitch a ride on a Tiger II heavy tank attached to* Kampfgruppe Peiper. *The* Kampfgruppe *was the spearhead of the 1st SS Panzer Division.*

RIGHT: *A King Tiger moves through the Ardennes up to the start line for Operation* Wacht am Rhein. *Note the paratrooper on the tank (third from left) equipped with the MP34/ StG44 assault rifle; a lightweight design that was copied after the war in weapons such as the AK-47.*

a significant waste of German resources. However, they had a quite dramatic effect upon American rear-area morale, out of all proportion to their numbers. Convinced that paratroops and commandos were swarming all over the Ardennes, dressed as GIs, American soldiers added to the confusion of the battle by stopping everyone they met and demanding proof of identity. As normal identity cards were no longer sufficient, such proof was usually demanded through the medium of 'catch questions,' and if any American did not know 'the capital of Illinois' or the title of 'the man between center and tackle of a line of scrimmage' he was instantly suspected. Even General Bradley was delayed in this way on one occasion, while Eisenhower, believed to be the object of a special assassination squad, was surrounded by so many security men that he was virtually a prisoner in his own HQ. If a major German breakthrough had occurred, such incidents could have had a decisive demoralizing effect. As it was, they were merely occasional irritants.

With the bulk of his infantry and all his 'specialist' units thus stalled or ineffective, Dietrich had no choice but to depend on his armor to achieve his aims. Two SS panzer divisions, the 12th on the right and 1st on the left, should have been committed by the end of the first day, exploiting gaps made in the American lines by the infantry and reaching the Meuse by 18 December. The failure of 12th SS Panzer against the 2nd and 99th Divisions was apparent relatively quickly, leading to its redeployment. This left the 1st to carry out the plan. Operating immediately behind 3rd Parachute Division, it should have been able to sweep through the Losheim

gap with ease. In the event a significant proportion of it, commanded by SS Obersturmbannführer Jochen Peiper, did manage to break through, but was not supported and, in the face of growing American defenses, was not decisive. Its story illustrates that essence of the Ardennes battle, with its mixture of confusion, harshness and small-unit action. Its failure also marks the end of Sixth Panzer Army's efforts in the north.

Peiper was a natural choice to lead the spearhead assault. A committed Nazi with a record of ruthless action on the Eastern Front, where his tank unit was known as the 'Blowtorch Battalion' after the destruction of two villages and their inhabitants, he was briefed for his part in *Wacht am Rhein* on 14 December. *Kampfgruppe Peiper* comprised 100 Mark IV and V (Panther) tanks, a battalion of 42 King Tigers and a fully motorized panzer grenadier unit (a force which constituted about half the total strength of 1st SS Panzer Division). Peiper was ordered to push through the southern sector of 99th Division's lines around Buchholz Station and Honsfeld, penetrate down the Amblève valley to its junction with the Salm River at Trois Ponts and then race through Werbomont to cross the Meuse at Huy. A rigid, unalterable route was to be followed to avoid blocking roads earmarked for 12th SS Panzer to the north and Peiper was given strict instructions to keep moving at all times, regardless of events on his flanks. The idea was not only to effect a breakthrough which could then be widened by the rest of 1st SS Panzer, but also to create maximum chaos deep in the American rear, a process which, on the evidence of traditional Blitzkrieg, would quickly lead to collapse.

From the start, things did not run smoothly. On 16 December, as *Kampfgruppe Peiper* approached its start

LEFT: *Members of the 1st SS Panzer Division check their position at a crossroads.*

RIGHT: *One of the worst atrocities committed in the West during the latter stages of the war occurred at Malmèdy. Over 80 unarmed US prisoners were shot by troops under the command of Major Josef Diefenthal.*

BELOW LEFT: *A German NCO passes orders to his comrades. In reality, this 'action' shot is a still from a German propaganda film. Of interest, however, is the US rainproof worn by the NCO, presumably 'liberated' from captured supplies.*

BELOW RIGHT: *The remains of a German convoy. Although poor weather kept Allied fighter-bombers on the ground during the initial stages of the operation, occasional breaks in the low cloud allowed some aircraft to carry out interdiction missions.*

line near Losheim, it became embroiled in the enormous traffic jam behind the German lines. Peiper had to force his way through, by-passing a destroyed railroad bridge which was one of the causes of the chaos, and did not reach the newly captured town of Lanzerath until nearly midnight. There he should have been briefed and aided by the 9th Parachute Regiment of 3rd Parachute Division, but it was soon obvious that that unit was poorly led and confused. Peiper had to take personal command, leading the paratroops and his own men in a successful assault on Buchholz Station early on 17 December. He then moved on to Honsfeld, entering the town unopposed by the simple expedient of tagging on to a disorganized American column. Once in the town, he ordered 9th Parachute Regiment to stay put and, gathering his *Kampfgruppe* around him, pushed on alone. He had successfully turned the southern flank of 99th Division and was already in the American rear. Breakthrough seemed assured.

According to his orders, Peiper should now have headed due west as quickly as possible, but he was already aware of another problem – his lack of fuel reserves. As a result he decided to disobey his instructions, and headed north for a US gasoline dump at Bullingen on the route ascribed to 12th SS Panzer. He helped himself to an estimated 50,000 gallons of gasoline before moving back on to the Ligneuville road, hoping to capture an antiaircraft brigade HQ at that town. To ensure success, Peiper split his force, sending the panzer grenadiers under Major Josef Diefenthal along the main road while he led the bulk of the armor to envelope Ligneuville from the south. The maneuver was carried out easily and, although the American HQ did manage to escape, both groups had joined up again in the town by late afternoon.

It was during the course of this advance that Diefenthal's force was responsible for one of the more shocking atrocities of the war in Western Europe - the Malmèdy Massacre. As the panzer grenadiers, with armor sup-

port, had followed the northern route to Ligneuville they had approached the vital crossroads at Baugnez, just south of Malmèdy, where they were to turn left to link up with Peiper. The road through to Ligneuville was packed with American traffic, much of it belonging to 7th Armored Division moving down from Ninth Army and, in order to clear a space, Diefenthal fired on the unfortunate 285th Field Artillery Observation Battalion. Lacking heavy weapons and incapable of stopping either tanks or half-tracks, about 120 men of that unit surrendered, whereupon they were herded into a nearby field and shot. Eighty-five unarmed, helpless prisoners of war did not survive. It was not the only atrocity committed by *Kampfgruppe Peiper* – American prisoners had already died at Bullingen, more were to be shot in Ligneuville and Stavelot – but it was the most sickening. The discovery of the unburied dead by other American units in the area later on 17 December was immediately publicized and probably did much to har-

LEFT: *Troops inspect a Tiger II, apparently abandoned by its crew when it ran out of petrol on the road to Stavelot.*

den defensive efforts throughout the Ardennes.

Peiper left Ligneuville at about 1700 hours on 17 December, aiming for the important bridge across the Amblève at Stavelot. The road was narrow and poor (Peiper was later to complain that his entire route was fit 'not for tanks but for bicycles') and American defenses were hurriedly being prepared. One of these – a roadblock by a cliff just to the east of Stavelot which could not be by-passed – proved to be of the utmost importance. Although manned by only 13 soldiers of Company C, 291st Combat Engineer Battalion, armed with only a few mines and a bazooka, it succeeded in delaying Peiper for a crucial 13 hours. As his lead tanks approached, one was stopped by a bazooka shot and Peiper withdrew. He did not resume his advance until 0800 hours on 18 December and although he was then able to take Stavelot, and the bridge without loss (it is presumed that the bridge demolitions were sabotaged

by a *Greif* commando unit), the delay enabled Hodges to redeploy 30th Infantry Division from the north against the penetration. It was the first of the American blocking moves.

Peiper had not broken through entirely, however, for he still needed to cross the Salm River at Trois Ponts if he was to take Werbomont and get to the Meuse. Once again he was stopped, this time by a small task force belonging to the 51st Engineer Battalion, ordered to Trois Ponts late on 17 December. Once in position, they set up roadblocks and prepared two of the three bridges, across the Amblève and the Salm, for demolition. Both were destroyed as Peiper approached, blocking his direct route and forcing him to turn north toward La Gleize. He was beginning to lose both momentum and the initiative, as he was forced to react to a series of American moves designed to blunt his advance and contain his force. His luck changed momentarily at Che-

LEFT: *US troops pass the remains of a Tiger II in the vicinity of Stavelot. This town saw bitter fighting in the first days of the German attack. Early on the morning of 19 December, elements of the US 117th Infantry Regiment retook the town, thereby ensuring the destruction of Kampfgruppe Peiper.*

RIGHT: *US ground troops survey the remains of a German mechanized column near Houffalize, a few miles to the north of Bastogne. Although difficult to distinguish, the remains in the left foreground are of a US halftrack, captured and pressed into service by the Germans.*

neux, southwest of La Gleize, where an intact bridge across the Amblève was found, but almost immediately he was hit by American fighter-bombers, operating through a rare break in the weather. By late afternoon on 18 December, therefore, *Kampfgruppe Peiper* had been located and checked. Elements of 30th Division were rushed to the area, preventing any movement westward across the Lienne creek, and by nightfall Peiper had no choice but to withdraw into La Gleize. Locating his men in that village and the neighboring one of Stoumont, he bivouacked for the night.

As Peiper rested, the remainder of 30th Division, aided by 82nd Airborne Division, newly released from strategic reserve by Eisenhower and redeployed to Werbomont while on their way to Bastogne, gradually closed in. Early in the morning of 19 December 1st Battalion, 117th Infantry (part of 30th Division), managed to recapture Stavelot, cutting Peiper off from the rear.

Counterattacks by the remainder of 1st SS Panzer, trying desperately to exploit the spearhead breakthrough, led to bitter fighting in Stavelot on 20 December, but the Americans held on. Peiper was now completely isolated. Over the next three days American units slowly squeezed the La Gleize-Stoumont pocket, employing artillery, armor and infantry in overwhelming numbers.

By 23 December, with his force decimated and out of gasoline, Peiper realized that all was lost and ordered a breakout on foot. Only a small proportion of his original *Kampfgruppe* survived to link up with friendly forces east of St Vith three days later. Sixth Panzer Army had run its course and, in the process, the Americans had built up a solid defensive line, facing south, from Elsenborn to Stoumont. The northern shoulder of the salient had been held. The German offensive was beginning to stall.

RIGHT: *US infantry, possibly members of the 30th Division, move up to Stavelot to complete the destruction of* Kampfgruppe Peiper. *By 23 December, with his forces out of food, fuel and ammunition, Peiper ordered them to break out on foot.*

3
ONSLAUGHT
IN THE NORTH

Dietrich's lack of progress was recognized by OKW as early as 20 December, and although it was never intended at this stage that his attack should be halted or his forces withdrawn, the emphasis of the assault was shifted to Manteuffel's army. Here the initial gains had been more dramatic, incorporating breakthroughs in two areas, on the right through 106th Division toward St Vith and on the left through 28th Division toward Bastogne. If Dietrich could not push through on the shortest route to the Meuse, it was therefore logical to reinforce Manteuffel in the hope that his forces could exploit the gaps and open up the battle. On 20 December Dietrich's II SS Panzer Corps (2nd and 9th SS Panzer Divisions) was shifted southward to follow routes already opened up around St Vith, while Hitler's strategic reserve brigades (*Führer Begleit* and *Führer Grenadier*) were earmarked to support the Fifth Panzer Army.

Manteuffel's breakthrough toward St Vith was by no means complete by this date. On 16 December his 18th *Volksgrenadier* Division had outflanked 106th Division in the Schnee Eifel and appeared to face little opposition in its projected sweep westward, yet four days later St Vith itself, defended by a hastily assembled collection of units centered upon 7th Armored Division, was still holding out. The existence of this 'fortified horseshoe' was to continue until 23 December, and although some German formations did by-pass it to both north and south, it stood like a rock which effectively broke the tide of the German advance for a full week. Even when 7th Armored Division and its attached units withdrew, they did so into a screen of strong well-ordered American regiments, rushed into the area to prevent a German exploitation. Such regiments had not been available during the first few days of the battle and without the defense of St Vith it is conceivable that Manteuffel would have made it to the Meuse, if not beyond. St Vith bought time in the northern sector and that time was not wasted.

As with so many other aspects of the Ardennes battle, early defensive efforts around St Vith was extemporized, using whatever forces were available, until more organized formations could be moved in. Thus, although 7th Armored Division was ordered to move south from Ninth Army late on 16 December, it did not begin to arrive at St Vith until 24 hours later, having been rerouted from its original destination of Bastogne by Middleton when he heard the news from the Schnee Eifel. During this crucial period Major General Jones, in his divisional HQ at St Vith, was forced to improvise an initial defense. As his three front-line regiments – the 422nd, 423rd and 424th – were still to the east and apparently surrounded (in the event a large proportion of the 424th was to escape westward), very few troops were immediately available. Those that were, comprising two engineer battalions, the 81st and 168th, and Jones' HQ companies, had to be organized into a scratch force. Under Lieutenant Colonel Tom Riggs, they moved due east toward Schönberg, about two miles out of town, to set up a roadblock through which, it was hoped, 7th Armored Division would attack to relieve the regiments in the Schnee Eifel. Riggs only got as far as Prümerberg, however, before he encountered German forces. There, on high ground overlooking Schönberg, his task force dug in.

Meanwhile, 7th Armored Division was not moving toward St Vith with a great deal of speed, for the closer to the area of battle they came, the more confusion they encountered. Led by Combat Command B (CCB) under Brigadier General Bruce Clarke (who arrived at Jones' HQ ahead of his troops early on 17 December), the division was delayed by traffic jams, particularly between Vielsalm and St Vith. It was split in two by Peiper's advance to Ligneuville and lost contact with its support

PREVIOUS PAGES: *Troop-laden jeeps and trucks loaded with supplies and ammunition move along wintery roads on their way to stem the German tide.*

LEFT: *A Kubelwagen drives round a stationary Panther. Worsening weather and increasingly determined US resistance prevented the German assault waves from reaching most of their first objectives.*

artillery. The first elements of CCB did not join their commander until about 1600 hours. They were immediately ordered east to join Riggs at the roadblock. At about the same time Brigadier General Robert W Hasbrouck, commanding 7th Armored Division as a whole, arrived to confer with Jones and Clarke. Instantly recognizing the extent and danger of the German attack, he decided not to order a counterattack against the Schnee Eifel but to concentrate on denying St Vith to the enemy. The decision broke the last of Jones' resolve – he now had the dubious distinction of having lost an entire division faster than any other American in history – and although he should, by virtue of his rank, have taken command of the defense, he sensibly handed it over to the infinitely more experienced Clarke. Hasbrouck agreed before moving back to set up divisional HQ at Vielsalm from where he could direct the battle as a whole. By the end of 17 December, therefore, defensive measures were beginning to take shape, principally to the east of St Vith where a fairly strong mix of armor and engineer-infantry, supported by a field artillery battalion (the 275th, available since the collapse of 14th Cavalry Group), was in position.

Fortunately for the Americans the next few days were not to see a concerted German effort against the town, which was by-passed as soon as its defense was recognized. Thus on 18 December probing attacks against the Prümerberg roadblock were beaten off, while to the north a potentially dangerous outflanking move by elements of 1st SS Panzer Division, advancing in support of *Kampfgruppe Peiper*, was countered by the commitment of Combat Command A (CCA) of 7th Armored Division around the village of Poteau. After hard fighting had persuaded the Germans that the Americans meant business, 1st SS Panzer decided to move westward, leaving St Vith to the infantry units which should have been following up. The fact that these units were still trying to break into defensive positions in front of the Elsenborn Ridge contributed significantly to the survival of St Vith.

The probing attacks continued on 19 December, but the lack of a decisive assault enabled Hasbrouck and Clarke to organize and consolidate their defenses. By this time the screen around St Vith was beginning to take on the appearance of a horseshoe with the open end facing west. In the north, between Vielsalm and Poteau, the defenses were light, for dense woods, made even more difficult to pass by the winter weather, acted as a useful barrier. Around Poteau itself CCA of 7th Armoured Division was in relatively strong positions, linked on their right to CCB and Riggs' task force on the high ground at Prümerberg. To their right, bending back slightly to the west, was CCB of 9th Armored Division, moved in by Middleton from his mobile reserve, together with the remnants of the 424th Infantry Regiment, recently extricated from the southern sector of the Schnee Eifel. Thereafter the flank was 'in the air,' although the gap was filled to a certain extent as far south as Trois Vierges when the 112th Regimental Combat Team (RCT), 28th Division, pushed northwestward by the German breakthrough on the Our River, suddenly appeared. It was closely followed by 116th Panzer Division, however, and gradually gave ground toward St Vith (thus completing the southern curve of the horseshoe) until the Germans decided to continue westward. Between Gouvry and Vielsalm there was no defense at all, it being hoped that other American units would be moved in from the west as a plug. If this did not happen, of course, it was also a useful escape route for the St Vith defenders. Finally, to bolster up the 424th Regiment and 112th RCT, Hasbrouck organized two mobile task forces, under Lieutenant Colonel Robert B Jones of the 814th Tank Destroyer Battalion and Captain Franklin P Lindsey of 14th Cavalry Group respectively, stationing them at Gouvry and Gruflange in the south. It was not an unbreachable defense – it was particularly vulnerable to encirclement and outflanking moves – but it was well organized and prepared. It was prepared only just in time.

The significance of St Vith altered dramatically on 20 December. Hitler's acceptance of Dietrich's failure and his decision to concentrate on Manteuffel's breakthroughs not only released fresh bodies of troops to add to the pressure but also made the capture of St Vith essential to the revised German plan. In American hands the town straddled vital north-south communications and acted as a block in the path of a broad advance. Under German control it would open up the northern approaches to Bastogne and, hopefully, break the logjam of American defense. As soon as he knew of Hitler's change of plan, therefore, Model ordered the swift destruction of Clarke's horseshoe, using 62nd and 560th *Volksgrenadier* Divisions as well as the *Führer Begleit* Brigade, released from OKW reserve. As an added bonus, he also received the 18th *Volksgrenadiers*,

ABOVE RIGHT: *The crew of an antitank gun wait to spring an ambush on a German armored column. Small teams, often armed with little more than a bazooka and a few mines, were able to slow the pace of the German advance.*

LEFT: *Troops of the 7th Armored Division move down the road to St Vith. The holding of this important communication center lasted until 23 December. The town was in fact supposed to fall on the first day of Operation* Wacht am Rhein *and it seems likely that if it had fallen the way to the Meuse would have been open.*

RIGHT: *Smiling GIs pull back to a new position in the face of the German onslaught. In most cases, as here, US withdrawals were carried out in an orderly manner.*

relieved of their mopping-up duties on the Schnee Eifel by the sudden surrender of the 422nd and 423rd Infantry Regiments late on 19 December, and could expect the arrival of II SS Panzer Corps as soon as it redeployed from Dietrich's sector. With such force beginning to concentrate against him and with elements of 1st SS Panzer and 116th Panzer by-passing to north and south, Clarke faced overwhelming odds.

The 20 December was a day of decision for the Allies as well. Even since the initial reports of the assault had trickled through to Eisenhower, the Supreme Commander and his staff had been aware of the need for fundamental command changes to deal with the situation. As Manteuffel's forces broke through they created a significant salient in the American lines (the 'Bulge' from which the popular name for the Ardennes battle comes), which threatened to split Bradley's 12th Army Group in two. Bradley's headquarters was situated in

Luxembourg, to the south of the salient. Communications all around the battle area were poor and control of the northern sector, by now in the process of being heavily reinforced to stop what the Allies imagined was a drive to Liège, was almost impossible. It therefore seemed logical to split the battle area in half along a line drawn between Givet in the west and Prüm in the east and give control of each sector to a different commander. The decision was made on 20 December and thereafter, for the duration of the battle, all forces north of the Givet-Prüm line (the entire Ninth Army and most of Hodges' First) were transferred to 21st Army Group under Montgomery, leaving Bradley to concentrate on the south. Militarily it was a sound move, although politically it did seem to cause the sort of inter-Allied squabbling which Hitler had planned to exploit. Montgomery's appointment was unpopular with many Americans, particularly when both he and the

British Press appeared to presume that the Ardennes front would have collapsed without his help, but it did rationalize the command structure. Once again, Hitler's presumption that the Allied reaction to *Wacht am Rhein* would be disjointed proved false.

Montgomery's new command area included St Vith and although his initial reaction was to order an immediate withdrawal of Clarke's forces to 'straighten the line,' he was persuaded that a defense of the horseshoe, however short, might impose some decisive delays upon the German advance. Consequently, late on 20 December, he ordered Ridgway's XVIII Airborne Corps at Werbomont to link up with Clarke using 82nd Airborne Division and a portion of 3rd Armored Division (the latter on attachment from VII Corps). Ridgway was to move into the gap between Vielsalm and Salmchâteau and keep it open as an escape route for 7th Armored Division, to be used after sufficient delay had been imposed on the Germans.

The Germans attacked St Vith in force on 21 December, concentrating on the routes from the east and north. Heavy fighting ensued in very poor weather conditions and, not surprisingly, the American defenses began to crack. First to go was the roadblock at Prümerberg, hit by sustained artillery fire and determined assaults from the 18th *Volksgrenadiers*. By the end of the day Riggs' task force had been split from CCA of 7th Armored Division and surrounded. Riggs attempted to break out to the west after dark, but deep snow hampered his progress and he was forced to surrender. Early the next morning the *Führer Begleit* Brigade followed up in the same area, penetrating deeply between CCB at Porteau and CCA to its right. Clarke abandoned St Vith, pulling back his left flank as far west as Hinder-

shausen, and asked for permission to withdraw. As Ridgway's forces had arrived at Vielsalm and Salmchâteau, Montgomery concurred, even though by now the battle area had been churned to mud, which made movement of any kind difficult.

Fortunately, by 0500 hours on 23 December, a sudden frost had hardened the ground and Clarke began to pull back. Protected by elements of 82nd Airborne Division, all the forces in the horseshoe had been successfully withdrawn by dusk, leaving the Germans in possession of St Vith and its surrounding area. It was a Pyrrhic victory, for although Model was now free to swing his divisions northwestward in a broad drive to the Meuse, American defenses had consolidated in his projected path. He was going to have to fight through them with exhausted troops.

German forces which had by-passed or were involved in the assault against St Vith – the infantry and armor of Manteuffel's right wing, plus some of the redeployed SS panzer units from Dietrich's army – were intent upon swinging toward the northwest, aiming for the Meuse between Huy and Liège. At the beginning of the battle this was an American rear area, virtually unprotected once the front line had been breached, and susceptible to the sort of panic and collapse which traditional Blitzkrieg caused. Fortunately for the Allies the successful holding action on the Elsenborn Ridge, together with the defense of St Vith for a week, prevented an immediate breakthrough and enabled the

LEFT: *An infantryman lays a mine by the side of a Belgium country road. Such devices could delay whole columns of German tanks if used correctly.*

RIGHT: *Members of an airborne division move to reinforce the defenders of St Vith.*

Americans to rush troops into the region in an attempt to create a defensive line. It was a crucial phase of the battle, developing into a race between American and German units to occupy key road networks and river crossings along an 80-mile front.

The area in question, running westward from the Elsenborn positions, is divided roughly down the middle by the River Salm. To the east of the river, following the Amblève valley to the original front line of 16 December, lay the sector which offered the quickest route to Liège, principally following the road through Malmèdy and Spa. This was the area which Dietrich had tried to break into on the first day, only to be stopped by the 2nd and 99th Divisions in front of Elsenborn. The western sector, bordered by the Salm on the east and the Ourthe on the west, offered a more usable road – Route 15, running from Bastogne, through Manhay and Werbomont, to Liège – but entailed potentially difficult river crossings and necessitated an early advance through the Losheim gap to the road network centered upon St Vith. Both sectors therefore had much to offer to the Germans, although American defensive measures did need to be preempted if the offensive was to regain its momentum.

LEFT: *A grenadier hugs the earth as a shell explodes in the near distance, sending up a plume of dense smoke.*

RIGHT: *An infantryman examines an abandoned M3 halftrack used by the Americans as an ambulance. Its seemingly good condition suggests it was ditched by its crew.*

By 20 December the Allied commanders were trying desperately to create such defenses before the panzers could outflank them. A degree of success had been achieved – 1st Division had moved into Elsenborn by 17 December, 30th Division had been deployed against Peiper's spearheads at Stavelot, Malmèdy and Stoumont by the 18th, and 82nd Airborne had been redeployed to the west of the Salm, with a Combat Command of 3rd Armored on its right, between the Salm and the Ourthe, by the 19th – but the line was thin and, as yet, uncoordinated. Continuing German attacks could still be successful, particularly if the vital crossroads at Malmèdy in the east and Manhay in the west could be taken, for they would crack the American positions on the northern flank wide open.

Assaults on the eastern sector, and especially against the approaches to Elsenborn on the shoulder of the developing bulge, had been intense since the opening of the battle, but they reached a new, almost desperate, level of ferocity in the early hours of 21 December. At 0130 hours elements of 12th SS Panzer Division, redeployed to widen the corridor created by 3rd Parachute

LEFT: *US gunners in action against a German troop concentration.*

RIGHT: *Wounded German prisoners are escorted to the rear, giving testament to the growing strength of the US reaction to their offensive.*

Division and *Kampfgruppe Peiper*, attacked the village of Don Burtgenbach from the direction of Bullingen, hoping to force a way into the Elsenborn defenses. They almost succeeded, hitting the 26th Infantry Regiment, 1st Division, with large numbers of tanks and infantry. However, the superior, and underestimated, flexibility of the Americans was beginning to tell. By this time the 1st, 2nd and 99th Divisions had decided to combine their artillery, with devastating results. The approaches to Don Burtgenbach were blasted in a massed artillery strike, disrupting the German attack and inflicting significant casualties. The 12th SS Panzer tried again 24 hours later, only to suffer the same fate, and thereafter the Elsenborn Ridge was not seriously assaulted. The shoulder was clearly secure.

A similar degree of defensive success was enjoyed at the same time around Malmèdy. After Peiper's forces had come perilously close to the town on 17 December, the 120th Infantry Regiment, 30th Division, had been moved in. They were attacked on 21 December by 150th Panzer Brigade, the unit formed by Skorzeny for rear-area disruption but now used conventionally in the

RIGHT: *A damaged halftrack left behind by the retreating Americans somewhere in the vicinity of Malmèdy.*

LEFT: *A blazing Sherman lies at the side of a road near the town of Manhay in Belgium. This strategically important town, lying on one of the most direct routes between Bastogne and Liège, was the scene of heavy fighting.*

absence of a massive breakthrough. A two-pronged advance, designed to isolate Malmèdy from east and west, failed in the face of determined resistance. As Peiper's spearhead had by this time been contained, the area east of the Salm was holding firm.

The western sector, between the Salm and the Ourthe, was less secure, however, for in the light of the initial attacks against the shoulder, fewer troops had been pushed into it during the early days. By 21 December therefore, despite the arrival of Ridgway's XVIII Airborne Corps HQ at Werbomont, little more than a division was protecting the region and even that was deployed more to maintain contact with St Vith than to consolidate an east-west line. The 82nd Airborne was occupying positions running principally north-south along the west bank of the Salm from Trois Ponts to Vielsalm, with only a few of its units projecting westward to just above Salmchâteau and Baraque de Fraiture. This meant that they were covering little over half the sector, leaving the area up to the Ourthe to a single Combat Command (CCR) of 3rd Armored Division, under Colonel Robert L Howze Jr. He established his HQ at Soy, to the west of Manhay, and divided his inadequate force into three groups, sending them to protect the river crossing at La Roche (Task Force Hogan), the Samrée to Soy road (Task Force Orr) and Manhey itself (Task Force Kane). Even as these dispositions were being made, on 20 December, the bulk of LVIII Panzer Corps (116th Panzer and 560th *Volksgrenadier* Divisions), having by-passed St Vith to the south, was taking Samrée, while 2nd SS Panzer Division, redeployed from Dietrich's reserve, was crossing the upper reaches of the Ourthe at Houffalize and advancing northward toward Manhay. CCR of 3rd Armored, overstretched and unsupported, was all that stood between the Germans and the Meuse.

The inevitable attacks began on 21 December but, remarkably, were held. The 116th Panzer, ordered to advance from Samrée toward a river crossing at Hotton, a few miles west of Soy, broke through the gap between Hogan and Orr but were stopped short of their objective by a scratch force of Howze's HQ troops. The Germans withdrew, convinced that a large American formation opposed them and shifted their probing assault to La Roche. Hogan's task force held out until the evening of 21 December, but was eventually forced to withdraw northward to Marcouray, allowing the panzers to cross the Ourthe on the 22nd. To the surprise of the Americans, who still saw Liège as the main German objective, the 116th then swung westward toward Dinant, leaving 3rd Armored in possession of their existing locations. This was just as well, for almost immediately 2nd SS Panzer attacked from Houffalize toward the crossroads at Baraque de Fraiture and the vital road junction of Manhay. The crossroads, defended by a hastily assembled rear-area force under Major Arthur C Parker III (and so, inevitably, known as 'Parker's Crossroads') and recently reinforced by a company of 325th Glider Infantry, 82nd Airborne Division, was hit by artillery, tanks and panzer grenadiers early on the morning of the 23rd. After an unequal struggle, the position fell, leaving the route to Manhay wide open.

Ridgway was now in a desperate situation, even when he received CCA of 3rd Armored as reinforcement, for his line was still extremely thin. Fortunately 2nd SS Panzer, finding that it was out on its own (too many German troops were involved in the final phases of the St Vith battle to offer support), did not exploit its success immediately. The pause was well-used by the Americans. On 24 December the survivors of St Vith were rested and, although the majority were in no condition to continue fighting, CCA of 7th Armored Division was still strong enough, on paper at least, to take over the defense of Manhay, joining Task Force Kane in plugging the gap. At the same time Montgomery ordered a 'straightening of the line,' withdrawing 82nd Airborne from Vielsalm-Salmchâteau to positions running east-west from Trois Ponts to Manhay and Hotton.

The 2nd SS Panzer renewed its attack at 2100 hours on 24 December (clearer weather was forcing the Germans to lie low during daylight for fear of Allied air

RIGHT: *US 155mm 'Long Toms' open fire during a night barrage against German positions.*

BELOW: *The remains of a German column, including a Panther, a Panzer IV and a captured US truck, outside a Belgian village, probably the victims of a strafing run by Allied ground-attack aircraft.*

attacks), advancing quite fortuitously straight down the interface between 3rd and 7th Armored Divisions. CCA of 7th Armored, exhausted after its gallant efforts around St Vith, broke under the pressure, leaving Kane isolated: Manhay fell. The panzers promptly moved westward to outflank 3rd Armored at Soy and to cross the river at Hotton. Ridgway, surprised at the lack of northward advance, took the opportunity to fill the Manhay gap by moving in the first units to arrive of the redeployed 75th Infantry Division. They were in position by the early hours of 25 December, so that when 2nd SS Panzer tried to widen the flank of its penetration, it made little headway. Ridgway completed his clocking move by ordering a scratch force of St Vith survivors (a combined CCA/CCB of 7th Armored together

with the 2nd Battalion, 424th Infantry Regiment) to retake Manhay, a task successfully carried out on the 26th. 2nd SS Panzer now had nowhere to go.

The Americans had thus managed, against considerable odds, to create a solid defensive line from Elsenborn all the way to Hotton. German attempts to swing northwestward to the Meuse had been blocked over an 80-mile front and if the maneuver was ever to be carried out it would have to be done by troops of Manteuffel's left wing, advancing by an extremely circuitous route from Bastogne in the south.

With clearer weather, increased Allied air activity and a chronic shortage of fuel on the German side, the odds in favor of this were never good. The Bulge was rapidly developing into a trap.

4
BASTOGNE UNDER SIEGE

By nightfall on 16 December the troops of General von Lüttwitz's XLVII Panzer Corps, responsible for the assault on Manteuffel's left wing, appeared to be on the verge of a breakthough. The initial infantry attacks, carried out by 26th *Volksgrenadier* Division, had crossed the Our, penetrated as far as Skyline Drive and punched large holes through Colonel Hurley Fuller's 110th Infantry Regiment. The 112th and 109th Regiments, to north and south respectively had held firm, but with the Our crossings secure von Lüttwitz was able to begin deployment of 2nd Panzer and Panzer *Lehr* Divisions during the hours of darkness. Their objectives were the bridges over the Clerf River, particularly at Clervaux and Drauffelt, the road center of Wiltz where Fuller had his HQ, and the approaches to Bastogne.

An early occupation of Bastogne was essential to German success, for the town was the focal point for seven major roads (leading to Houffalize in the north, St Vith in the northeast, Luxembourg in the southeast, Arlon in the south, Neufchâteau in the southwest and Marche and La Roche in the northwest). Its importance was recognized during the planning stages of *Wacht am Rhein*, when OKW officers had managed to persuade Hitler to exempt the town from his 'no deviation' rule, for if the Americans held on, the entire road network of the Ardennes, so crucial in an advance through winter weather, would be denied. According to the plan, 26th *Volksgrenadiers* were to capture Bastogne by the third day of the assault, allowing 2nd Panzer and Panzer *Lehr* to by-pass it to north and south, using roads free from American interference. It was an ambitious schedule, particularly as the *Volksgrenadiers* were also responsible for the Our and Clerf crossings, but during the first few days of the battle, it was very nearly realized.

The first priorities on 17 December were for XLVII Panzer Corps to clear the area east of Bastogne and for the panzer divisions to begin a rapid exploitation of the Meuse. In both respects a degree of success was enjoyed. Despite a gallant counterattack by elements of the 110th Regiment east of Clervaux, 2nd Panzer captured the town by late afternoon, crossing the Clerf and heading for Houffalize preparatory to a swing northwestward, toward the Meuse. The 110th Regiment thereby ceased to exist and, as the gap left by it became apparent, the other units of 28th Division were forced to pull back: the 112th Regiment toward St Vith and the 109th toward 4th Division on the southern flank of the assault area. The latter movement allowed Panzer *Lehr* to cross the Clerf at Drauffelt and 5th Parachute Division (on the right wing of Brandenberger's Seventh Army) to deploy west of the Our. Both units joined 26th *Volksgrenadiers* in an attack against Wiltz and when the town fell on 19 December, the southern approaches to Bastogne lay open. A major German breakthrough seemed inevitable.

The Americans had not been slow to appreciate the danger. General Middleton, whose corps HQ was in Bastogne, had begun defensive deployments as early as 17 December, sending two task forces from his mobile reserve (CCR of 9th Armored Division) to cover the eastern approaches to the town. Task Force Harper (under Lieutenant Colonel R S Harper) had established a roadblock at Allenborn, on the road to St Vith, while Task Force Rose (under Captain L K Rose) had moved a few miles to the northeast, protecting the route from Clervaux and Trois Vierges. At the same time a thin defensive screen had been set up in an arc from Foy to Neffe, covering the northeast to the rear of Harper and Rose and manned by hastily-collected units of the 128th

PAGES 50-51: *Members of a howitzer battery prepare for action.*

RIGHT: *The scene in the center of Bastogne as the German forces place the town under siege – refugees, with their pathetic bundles of clothing, attempt to escape the fighting.*

Combat Engineer Group. Task Force Harper did not survive for long. It was overrun by spearheads of 2nd Panzer Division late on 18 December, but as the Germans were intent upon exploitation toward Noville and Houffalize in the northwest, Bastogne itself was not directly threatened. This gave Middleton time to deploy the reinforcements being rushed to him under orders from the Supreme Commander.

The first of these formations to arrive was the CCB of 10th Armored Division under Colonel William L Roberts, released from Patton's Third Army by Eisenhower late on 16 December. As the troops drove into

LEFT: *While an officer scans the horizon for signs of the enemy, a US transport column, led by a Stuart light tank, falls back to a new defensive line.*

RIGHT: *German prisoners bring in a wounded comrade during the bitter fighting around St Vith.*

Bastogne 48 hours later, they were divided into three 'teams' and hurriedly sent out to form strongpoints in an arc to the east. Team O'Hara (Lieutenant Colonel James O'Hara) pushed southeast to an area around Wardin on the Luxembourg road, Team Cherry (Lieutenant Colonel Henry T Cherry) moved toward Longvilly on the route to St Vith in the east, and team Desobry (Major William R Desobry) traveled northeast to Noville on the road to Houffalize. They were supported by elements of 101st Airborne Division, under temporary command of Brigadier General Anthony C McAuliffe (the official divisional commander, Major General Maxwell D Taylor, was absent on leave), redeployed from their initial destination of Werbomont as soon as the threat became apparent. The first unit to arrive, the 501st Parachute Infantry Regiment, was sent due east, toward Team Cherry on the Longvilly road, late on 18 December. Unknown to them, spearheads of Panzer *Lehr* had already cut that road at Margeret, forming a solid block between the two American formations. The paratroops of the 501st were therefore stopped early on 19 December at Neffe and Team Cherry was forced to attempt a withdrawal to link up. Results were mixed. Team Cherry was caught in the open to the east of Neffe and destroyed, but the 501st, in a classic three-battalion attack, managed to push Panzer *Lehr* units out of Bizory to the north of Margeret, consolidating a defensive line which was to hold firm until the following day. Elsewhere the situation was much the same. In the northeast Team Desobry, supported by the 506th Parachute Infantry Regiment, beat off an attack by 2nd Panzer Division at Noville, while Team O'Hara was forced to give some ground including Wardin itself, in the southeast. The Germans were clearly probing for weak spots, but a coherent defensive line was beginning to emerge by the end of 19 December. The period of American confusion, during which the major German advances should have been made, was already coming to an end.

This was seen to good effect elsewhere on the same day, for while the defenders of Bastogne were sorting

themselves out, top-level Allied commanders at a meeting in Verdun were making some far-reaching strategic decisions. Eisenhower was by now convinced that the only way to destroy the German assault was to contain it between the already-solidifying shoulders around Elsenborn and Echternach, preparatory to counterattacks from north and south. Bastogne was the key, so priority had to be given to the south flank. Toward this end, the Supreme Commander canceled Patton's projected attack in the Saar and extended the front to be defended by 6th Army Group northward. The Third Army, thus released from both offensive and defensive commitments, could then turn north, toward Bastogne. Patton had already appreciated this, and when Eisenhower directed him to redeploy on 19 December, he was able to oblige with remarkable speed. The 4th Armored Division was ordered to move toward Arlon and 80th Infantry Division toward Luxembourg, while 26th Infantry Division was directed to concentrate as a re-

LEFT: *Men of the 501st Parachute Infantry Regiment, a unit of the 101st Airborne Division, move out of Bastogne on their way to Margeret, 18 December 1945. In a classic three-battalion attack, the regiment managed to push elements of Panzer* Lehr *out of Bizory, north of Margeret, buying time to organize the defenses of Bastogne.*

LEFT: *Brigadier General Anthony McAuliffe, temporary commander of the 101st Airborne Division, coordinated the defense of Bastogne.*

RIGHT: *The strain of battle is clearly etched on the faces of these two tired members of the 101st Airborne Division.*

serve, facing north. All three formations were earmarked for an advance toward Bastogne. Once again, American flexibility under pressure was superb.

Patton's forces could not be expected to begin their advance until 22 December at the earliest, so the Bastogne defenders still faced a difficult task against progressively stronger German assaults. On 20 December Team Desobry (now under Major Robert F Harwick of 101st Airborne since Desobry had been wounded the previous evening) came under sustained pressure from panzer grenadiers of 2nd Panzer Division, and although the initial attacks were repulsed, the American positions rapidly became untenable. Harwick was ordered to withdraw to link up with the 502nd Parachute Infantry Regiment to his south, a movement completed by 1700 hours. 2nd Panzer, unopposed, swept through Noville to Ortheuville and crossed the Ourthe River, outflanking Bastogne to the north. At the same time Panzer *Lehr* units managed to dislodge the paratroops of the 501st from their positions in Bizory in the east, forcing them back to within two miles of Bastogne itself. Brigadier General McAuliffe, appointed that day to command all American units involved in the defense, seemd to be facing a crisis.

Fortunately for the Americans the following day – 21 December – saw an easing of German pressure. This was partly due to a temporary break in the weather which allowed Allied aircraft to fly in supplies and hit ground targets, but it was also an indication of von Lüttwitz's growing frustration. Bastogne should have

RIGHT: *A machine-gun position somewhere in the vicinity of Bastogne. The severity of the conditions is evident.*

LEFT: *C-47 Dakotas drop supplies to the beleaguered garrison of Bastogne on 20 December. A break in the weather allowed this vital operation to go ahead.*

fallen on the 18th yet, despite panzer division break-throughs to north and south, the town's defenses were still holding out, principally in an arc from Noville to Wardin. He therefore spent the day reorganizing his forces, sending the bulk of Panzer *Lehr* to the south of Bastogne but keeping back the 901st Panzer Grenadier Regiment as a reinforcement to 26th *Volksgrenadiers*, now charged with taking the town. In addition, he shifted the emphasis of attack from the east right round to the southwest and west, a policy which completed the encirclement of American defense. The siege of Bas-

togne began late on 21 December, with the odds theoretically in the Germans' favor. The 2nd Panzer was cutting off communications to the north and Panzer *Lehr* and 5th Parachute Division, newly positioned astride the Arlon road, were in the south. Therefore, 26th *Volksgrenadiers*, comprising a reconnaissance battalion, an engineer battalion, the 39th, 77th and 78th *Volksgrenadier* Regiments as well as the 901st Panzer Grenadiers, could devote all its energies to a quick victory. Opposing them, under McAuliffe, there were four airborne regiments (501st, 502nd and 506th Parachute

LEFT: *Chow time for a group of GIs. Hot food could do much to restore the morale of cold and exhausted troops.*

RIGHT: *US groundcrew remove snow and ice from the fuselages of ground-attack aircraft in preparation for a sortie against German mechanized units.*

RIGHT: *US groundcrew remove snow and ice from the fuselages of ground-attack aircraft in preparation for a sortie against German mechanized units.*

and 327th Glider Infantry), four light artillery and two medium howitzer battalions, the 420th Armored Field Artillery Battalion, about 40 medium tanks and the 705th Tank Destroyer Battalion. They could not be expected to hold out.

Bearing this in mind, the commander of the 26th *Volksgrenadiers*, General Heinz Kokott, offered to negotiate the surrender of the town early on 22 December. McAuliffe's terse reply – 'Nuts!' – has entered the folklore of the Ardennes battle, but it was indicative of the high morale enjoyed by the American defenders at

this time. This was doubtless reinforced by news that Patton's counterattack had begun the same morning and was manifested in successful actions against Kokott's troops in the south around Assenois and in the northwest around Champs. Once these attacks had been repulsed, Kokott seemed prepared to go over to the defensive, aiming for an investment of the town rather than a costly occupation. For this reason the next two days were relatively quiet. On 23 December limited German operations against Flamierge in the northwest and Marvie in the southeast were countered in im-

RIGHT: *Two infantrymen, their faces still covered with camouflage cream, discuss a recent patrol of the German positions around Bastogne.*

LEFT: *Wrecked and abandoned Panthers litter a field somewhere in southern Belgium.*

proving weather conditions (the same freeze which enabled Clarke to escape from St Vith), and a major Allied airlift began. This continued on the 24th, together with ground-attack air strikes which succeeded in preventing further German assaults. McAuliffe used the lull to rationalize his perimeter, drawing back the units deployed in a vulnerable salient around Flamierge and Marde St Etienne in the northwest. The ring of defenses around Bastogne was now only 16 miles in circumference.

Kokott resumed his offensive on Christmas Day, having been reinforced by elements of 15th Panzer Grenadier Division, taken from Manteuffel's reserve specially for operations against Bastogne. A major attack began to develop around Champs as early as 0300 hours. The plan was for the 77th *Volksgrenadier* Regiment to attack to the northwest of the village and tie down American units, whereupon the 115th Panzer Grenadier Regiment would break through to Hemroulle and into Bastogne itself. At first a degree of success was achieved – by 0530 hours the 77th had made a significant penetration and the 115th had overrun two

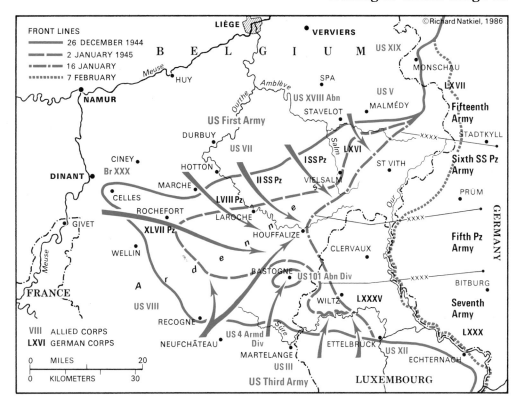

FRONT LINES
— 26 DECEMBER 1944
— 2 JANUARY 1945
— 16 JANUARY
— 7 FEBRUARY

©Richard Natkiel, 1986

VIII ALLIED CORPS
LXVI GERMAN CORPS

companies of the 327th Glider Infantry – but then disaster struck. As the panzer grenadiers moved in a pincer assault on Hemroulle they were caught in a specially prepared trap. As paratroops of the 502nd picked off the infantry with small-arms fire, the 705th Tank Destroyer Battalion took on the tanks. The German forces were wiped out, losing a total of 17 AFVs, and the attack ground to a halt. The immediate threat to Bastogne diminished as Kokott counted the cost, although, in the absence of a link up with Patton's force from the south, the town was still not secure.

Patton had worked hard since 19 December to organize his counterattack. The three divisions initially moved northward toward the Ardennes sector – 4th Armored, 26th and 80th Infantry – were quickly formed into III Corps under Major General John Millikin and given the main task of relieving Bastogne. At the same time, however, Major General Manton Eddy's XII Corps (10th Armored – less CCB – and 4th and 5th Infantry Divisions) was prepared for a drive on the right toward the Sûre River north of Ettelbrück. It was envisaged that this attack would eventually lead to

LEFT: *Infantry of the 10th Armored Division advance in open order toward an enemy position already under fire from heavy artillery. The division was committed to the operation to relieve Bastogne.*

RIGHT: *Tanks of the US 6th Armored Division deploy for action. Elements of the division played a key role in the siege of Bastogne.*

LEFT: *Paratroopers of the 82nd Airborne Division gather round the welcome warmth of a small fire after an evening patrol.*

Wiltz and even St Vith. This increased the workload on Patton's staff and, when combined with a total lack of knowledge about German dispositions, served to delay the start of the offensive until 22 December. Nevertheless, hopes ran high of an early link up with McAuliffe.

In the event, things did not go smoothly. Despite an initial advance all along the line of about seven miles on the first day, most of this proved to be over the no man's land between the opposing forces and as more difficult ground was encountered, particularly in the east

LEFT: *Weary and dejected German prisoners are lined up prior to being escorted into captivity.*

toward the Sûre River, the advance rapidly bogged down. The 4th Armored Division, operating on the extreme left and charged with responsibility for the actual relief of Bastogne, found the going especially hard. The division was divided as was normal practice, into three combat commands, of which two (CCA and CCB) were expected to attack while the third (CCR) was held in reserve. On 22 December CCA took the right wing of the advance, operating along the Arlon-Bastogne road, while CCB followed secondary roads to the west emanating from Habay La Neuve, aiming to converge with CCA as Bastogne was approached. Little opposition was encountered to begin with, but by noon on the first day both commands had made contact with units of 5th Parachute Division. CCB had to fight its way through Burnon – an operation which took until the early hours of the 23rd – while CCA was forced to redeploy against entrenched opposition at Martelange. The attacks seemed in danger of petering out well short of their objective.

When a similar pattern of slow, costly advance was experienced on Christmas Eve, Millikin was forced to act. He reinforced both commands with infantry drawn from 80th Division and, more importantly, deployed CCR of 4th Armored to the west of CCB, on the Neufchâteau-Bastogne road. This was an astute move, for when CCR advanced from Cobreville toward Remonville on the morning of 25 December, significant advances were made. A bitter battle had to be fought in Remonville itself, but by dusk on Christmas Day the way was clear to Remichampagne, Clochimont and Bastogne. Twenty-four hours later the first tanks broke through to link up with McAuliffe's troops and the siege was over. With contact now regained, a dangerous salient had been forced across the German line of

advance, threatening the security of those forces already heading westward. It was a turning point in the battle which, in conjunction with other events taking place at the same time, ensured eventual Allied victory.

ABOVE RIGHT: *Members of the 101st Airborne Division dig their comrades out of the remains of a bombed-out building in the center of Bastogne.*

RIGHT: *An historic moment – press photographers record the meeting of officers involved in the siege and relief of Bastogne. Curious civilians look on with some bemusement.*

5
COUNTING
THE COST

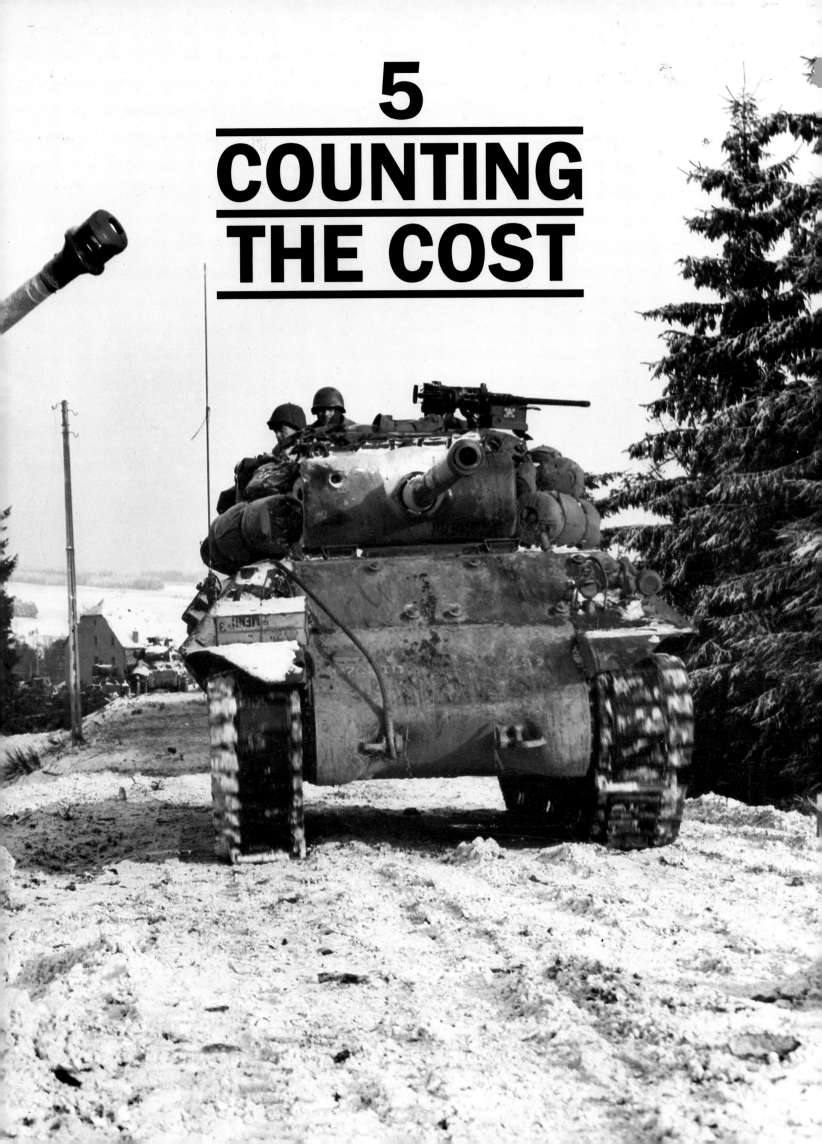

The by-passing of Bastogne by 2nd Panzer Division to the north and Panzer *Lehr* to the south – a process well under way by 20-21 December – presented the Americans with a potentially dangerous situation. The battle area as a whole was in a state of considerable confusion, with holding actions being fought at Elsenborn, La Gleize, St Vith, Bastogne and on the southern shoulder, but with large, relatively undefended gaps in between. Admittedly the Germans were being slowed down – to a decisive extent as it turned out – but an advance to the Meuse was still a distinct possibility. Once the panzers broke loose to the west, blocking moves at places such as Bastogne could become irrelevant, tying down valuable resources at a time when as many troops as possible would be needed in a mobile defensive role. It was therefore something of a gamble when Middleton, after consultation with his superiors, allowed McAuliffe to become encircled late on 21 December for, in reality, he had little left with which to prevent a panzer advance. Reserves moved into the battle area had been devoted to the defense either of key locations or of the line from Elsenborn to the Ourthe, leaving a significant gap between that river and the Meuse at Dinant. If German forces, probably from XLVII Panzer Corps in the south, as all others had been or were in the process of being blocked, could swing into this gap, capturing the Ourthe river crossing at Hotton and the important road junction at Marche on Route 35,

the way would be clear to Liège and the Allied rear, east of the Meuse. The first priority should therefore have been a rapid expansion of the northern defensive line westward, to close the gap, but with the heavy commitment of reserves elsewhere and a degree of Allied confusion about German aims, this was not an easy policy to carry out.

By 20 December most of the Allied commanders were convinced that the German plan was to swing northward to Liège, cutting off the left wing of Hodges' First Army facing the Siegfried Line; in other words, Rundstedt's 'little slam' strategy, rejected by Hitler earlier in the month. With this in mind, it was expected that all the German assault formations, once having broken through, would take the shortest route to Liège, cutting northward somewhere between Elsenborn and the Ourthe, ignoring Dinant and Namur to the northwest. Thus, although significant countermoves were initiated as early as 19 December, when Montgomery redeployed Horrocks' XXX Corps from Holland to an area between Brussels and Liège and Hodges withdrew Collins' VII Corps from Düren in the north to the Marche Plain, west of the Ourthe, there appeared to be little sense of urgency involved. Both were regarded as long-term moves, the former to create a defense in depth and the latter to begin the build up of a counterattack force designed to advance eastward, across the main German thrusts. The development of panzer attacks toward

PAGES 62-63: *A tank-destroyer of the US 3rd Armored Division rolls past a crippled Panzer IV to the south of Langlir, 13 January 1945. The panzer is fitted with a band of spaced armor around its turret as improved protection against antitank rounds.*

RIGHT: *Vehicles of the US 4th Armored Division move past the body of an American infantryman, probably the victim of a mine or artillery fire.*

Dinant and Namur, at right angles to the imagined German axis, was therefore something of a surprise, necessitating a hurried and piecemeal commitment of Collins' corps to close the Ourthe-Meuse gap.

Collins had been given four divisions with which to prepare his counterattack, but they were by no means a coherent force on 20 December. The 2nd Armored and 84th Infantry were situated on the front line around Düren, so they had to be withdrawn and sent south over poor roads in winter conditions. The 3rd Armored was split up and already involved in the battle on the northern sector of the Ardennes; CCA was chasing von der Heydte's paratroops around Baraque Michel, CCB was attached to 30th Division for operations against *Kampfgruppe Peiper*, and CCR was moving into defensive positions east of the Ourthe. The 75th Infantry was

LEFT: *The imposing bulk of the Tiger II is clear from this photograph. Although armed with the uprated 8.8cm KWK43 gun and fitted with hull armor up to 150mm thick, this potent weapon suffered from being fitted with an unsuitable powerplant.*

RIGHT: *German troops captured by the 82nd Airborne Division are lined up by the side of a road near the Belgian town of Hierlot.*

LEFT: *Units of the 87th Infantry Division enter the town of St Hubert, shortly after it had been abandoned by its German defenders. St Hubert lies on the direct route from Bastogne to Dinant.*

an inexperienced formation which had to be moved into the area from Hodges' reserve. Furthermore, as Collins' HQ also had to be moved south to its new location, those units which did arrive were placed temporarily under Ridgway's command, a policy which inevitably led to their use wherever the danger was greatest. Thus, for example, when the first elements of 75th Infantry came within XVIII Airborne Corps area on 25 December they were immediately committed to the defense of Manhay, east of the Ourthe, rather than to the Ourthe-Meuse gap. In the end, this important sector was covered by 2nd Armored and 84th Infantry only, occupying a series

of strongpoints rather than a continuous line. The first units of 84th Infantry, 334th and 335th Infantry Regiments, in fact arrived on 21 December – a remarkable achievement in the prevailing conditions. They were deployed in battalion groups on the road between Hotton and Marche, with one battalion moving down to Rochefort, eight miles southwest of Marche, the following day. They were only just in time.

Responsibility for capturing Marche and opening the route to Namur lay with 2nd Panzer Division, aided on their left by Panzer *Lehr* and on their right by 116th Panzer from LVIII Panzer Corps. By 22 December all

LEFT: *Infantry and tanks of the 75th Division move forward to engage German forces blocking the route to Houffalize to the north of Bastogne.*

three divisions were converging on the Ourthe-Meuse gap, having successfully by-passed the defensive blocks at Bastogne and St Vith. The 2nd Panzer was in the lead, pushing hard toward its objective despite a number of Allied air strikes against its lead formations. Indeed, so intent were they upon exploitation that they skirted Marche to the south, leaving the capture of the town to a detached panzer grenadier group, and headed straight for the Meuse. It was an ill-considered move, placing them between Marche to the north and Rochefort to the south, each defended by a relatively strong American force. When the lead units encountered probing Allied patrols late on 22 December they halted in a dangerously vulnerable 'finger' protruding northwestward for nearly seven miles. Nor were they fully supported on their flanks; Panzer *Lehr* was meeting opposition from the defenders of Rochefort while 116th Panzer was finding the going hard between Hotton and Verdenne. The 2nd Panzer Division was occupying a potential trap.

This seems to have been realized by the Germans before the Americans, for throughout 23-24 December enormous efforts were made to broaden the finger. They were not very successful. On the left, after heavy fighting, Panzer *Lehr* units managed to capture Rochefort, only to be held to the west at Ciergnon as they tried to link up with 2nd Panzer. The 116th Panzer on the right had no better luck, finding it impossible to break through the 84th Infantry defenses between Hotton and Verdenne and reinforcement divisions – 9th Panzer and the bulk of 15th Panzer Grenadier – were kept away from the area by Allied air attacks. By late afternoon on the 24th, 2nd Panzer – by now running desperately short of fuel – should have been ordered to withdraw but, despite pleas from von Lüttwitz, Hitler characteristically refused permission. The lead units, occupying two separate areas, one around the village of Foy-Notre-Dame and the other around Celles and Conjoux, all within four miles of the Meuse, prepared for the inevitable American attack.

This did not materialize immediately. The first units

of 2nd Armored Division, commanded by Major General Ernest N Harman, had arrived north of Marche as early as 22 December, but had received little information about either their role or the German dispositions. Harman therefore spent two days feeling his way, linking up with elements of the British XXX Corps on his right and sending probing patrols of his CCA southward from Ciney toward Rochefort, and it was not until late on 24 December that the vulnerability of 2nd Panzer was realized. Even then, a counterattack against the finger was by no means automatic, for with defense as the first priority Harman could find no one among his superiors

ABOVE RIGHT: *Units of the 90th Infantry Division move through the main street of Bastogne during the push to eradicate the German lodgment in the Ardennes.*

RIGHT: *C-47s fly in supplies to forces engaged in the advance from Bastogne. In the foreground a Sherman tank fires on an already burning target.*

LEFT: *Wearing white sheets as rudimentary winter camouflage, three GIs move out on patrol.*

prepared to sanction an offensive, however limited or guaranteed of success. In the end, he used a considerable amount of personal initiative, based upon the ambiguity of his orders, and moved cautiously forward early on Christmas Day. CCB of 2nd Armored advanced southwestward from Ciney in two columns, one through Achêne and Le Hoiusse on the right and the other through Conneux and Conjoux on the left, aiming to link up at Celles. At the same time, CCA moved down the Rochefort road to cut the base of the finger. The results were spectacular. By the end of the day 2nd Panzer's reconnaissance battalion at Foy-Notre-Dame

had been eliminated and the encirclement of Celles virtually achieved. Desperate attacks by Panzer *Lehr* and 9th Panzer, designed to keep open the route to Celles, had failed. The 2nd Panzer was nearing the end of the road.

The Celles pocket was finally closed early on 26 December, whereupon the reunited CCB, aided by Allied air strikes, turned back on itself to destroy the trapped formations. By dusk the bulk of 2nd Panzer, comprising the 304th Panzer Grenadier Regiment, two battalions of the 3rd Panzer Regiment, three artillery battalions and the majority of the divisional anti-

LEFT: *A Sherman tank maintains the momentum of the US counterattack in the Ardennes. Although much hard fighting remained, by the beginning of January 1945 the German offensive had been contained.*

RIGHT: *Carefully sited to cover a long stretch of straight road, this 57mm antitank gun team prepares to deal with a localized German attack.*

aircraft, had ceased to exist. The tip of the bulge had been blunted.

General Bradley described 26 December as the day on which the 'high-water mark' of the German offensive was reached and viewing the battlefield in its entirety, no one would dispute his judgment. All along the northern flank, between Elsenborn and Dinant, the panzer assaults had been stopped and a solid defensive line created. In the south the siege of Bastogne had been lifted and a narrow corridor punched through to connect Third Army with McAuliffe's men and to interdict the lines of panzer advance in the southern sector. The battle was by no means over, particularly around Bastogne, but the Bulge had been contained and the Germans forced on to the defensive. The initiative was about to pass into American hands.

Though in retrospect 26 December may be viewed as a turning point, there must have been little direct evidence of it at the time in the foxholes and ruins of the Ardennes. Admittedly news of the destruction of 2nd Panzer Division did cause Hitler to authorize a withdrawal of Panzer *Lehr* and 116th Panzer units to a more defensible line, but the Führer had not abandoned the offensive entirely. He was convinced that operations

RIGHT: *US soldiers search the war-torn village of Wiltz in Luxembourg for German snipers. Wiltz fell in the early stages of* Wacht am Rhein *but was abandoned by the Germans in mid-January 1945.*

since 16 December had disrupted the Allies and delayed their assault on the Rhine by weeks if not months. He insisted that Manteuffel's forces should regroup and concentrate on the elimination of the Bastogne salient preparatory to a renewed drive through the Ourthe-Meuse gap, still with Antwerp as the ultimate objective. At the same time, in an effort to increase the pressure on the Allied High Command, he ordered Army Group G, deployed to the south facing a line from Metz to Strasbourg, to prepare an assault upon Devers' overstretched 6th Army Group. There was clearly a large amount of hard fighting still to be done. German defeat was by no means a foregone conclusion.

The 'master stroke' was in fact closer to success in one respect than even Hitler realized, for although the reaction of the Allies to the *Wacht am Rhein* offensive had been far faster and better coordinated than originally predicted by OKW, a serious rift between top commanders in the Anglo-American camp reached crisis proportion in late December and early January. The strategic arguments over narrow- or broad-front advance after the Normandy breakout had never been adequately solved. Montgomery particularly remained convinced that a concentration of resources under a single land command, subordinate only to the Supreme Commander, should be ordered on the Allied left, against the Ruhr and North German Plain. His beliefs were reinforced after his appointment to command the northern sector of the Bulge, for he saw the transfer of the US First and Ninth Armies to 21st Army Group as the first step in this direction, regardless of the temporary nature of the arrangement. The crisis reached its apogee on 30 December when, in a remarkable letter to Eisenhower, Montgomery spoke openly of the need for 'one commander . . . to direct and control' all land operations in northwest Europe, and virtually insisted that this should be himself as 'C in C, 21st Army Group.'

ABOVE LEFT: *An exhausted German soldier takes shelter behind a hedge. By late December the initiative in the battle had finally passed to the Americans, and the Germans were forced to make more defensive moves.*

LEFT: *German prisoners raise a smile for the camera while their grim-faced guard looks on.*

RIGHT: *A GI helps to process some of the 50,000 German troops taken in the Battle of the Bulge. Here, he is checking identification papers.*

Eisenhower read this as an ultimatum and was on the verge of referring the whole affair to the Combined Chiefs of Staff in a report which would have offered them a choice between himself and Montgomery. As confidence in the Supreme Commander was high in Washington, it began to look as if Montgomery would be forced to resign, an action charged with enormous implications for continued Anglo-American cooperation. It was just what Hitler wanted.

Fortunately for the Allies the day was saved by Major General Francis de Guingand, Chief of Staff to 21st Army Group who, after having been warned by a British liaison officer at Bradley's HQ about what was happening, spent the next two days patching things up. After a visit to Eisenhower in Paris on 30 December, during which he persuaded the Supreme Commander to delay sending his report, de Guingand flew to Montgomery's HQ at Tongres on the 31st and explained the magnitude of the crisis to his superior. Montgomery, genuinely surprised at the furore caused by what he termed 'frank remarks,' immediately wrote an apology to Eisenhower, pledging his loyalty and support, and

RIGHT: *A US NCO reads a message scrawled on a wall in a village to the north of Clervaux. It reads: 'Behind the last battle of this war stands our victory.'*

the crisis blew over. It was only a temporary *rapprochement*, for at a Press conference on 7 January 1945 relations were soured yet again when Montgomery, unintentionally but tactlessly, overstated the part played by himself and his British troops in the Ardennes battle. The British newspapers picked this up and gave it great prominence, with headlines proclaiming that Montgomery 'foresaw the attack' (when Bradley quite patently did not) and that he 'saved the day' as Middleton's VIII Corps collapsed. Inter-Allied relations reached a new low and, although once again the rift was healed by some hasty diplomatic actions on both sides, it was obvious that the British and American commanders were by no means united. The only consolation was that all this took place after the 'high-water mark' of the German offensive had passed, so denying the enemy any advantage.

Meanwhile the fighting in the Ardennes sector continued with undiminished ferocity, with the emphasis firmly on the Bastogne salient. Although McAuliffe and Millikin had managed to link up on 26 December the corridor created by 4th Armored Division was narrow and extremely tenuous; attracting forces from both the opposing armies like a magnet. Just as the Allied priority was to expand and consolidate this link, turning Bastogne into a springboard for an offensive to the north and east, so that German aims were to cut the corridor, eliminate the American defense and clear the way for a fresh offensive toward the west. What had been a diffuse and widespread battle was suddenly concentrated into a relatively small area in the southern sector.

The initial American moves were made on 28 December. Eisenhower spend much of that day conferring with Montgomery about the organization of a counter-attack from the north, designed to link up with Patton's army at Houffalize and so split the Bulge down the middle, but when it became apparent that regrouping would take at least until 3 January, he shifted his attention to the south. By this time a new strategic reserve had been created, comprising the 11th Armored and 87th Infantry Divisions, and this was immediately released to help in the expansion of the Bastogne corridor. Patton deployed the new troops to the west of the original breakthrough line, aiming to use them to flush out the salient toward Flamierge and Champs, timing their advance to coincide with one by 35th Infantry Division in the east, driving toward Margaret and Longvilly. If all three divisions could push forward until they were in line with 101st Airborne, still protecting Bastogne itself, then a solid wedge would be established deep into the enemy flank, enabling 26th Infantry Division, even farther to the east, to advance to Wiltz or even Clervaux. The attacks were scheduled to begin in the early hours of 30 December.

They met with little success, smashing straight into the flanks of German assault formations attempting to cut the corridor from west and east. The 11th Armored Division, with 87th Infantry on its left, hit and was hit by elements of Panzer *Lehr* and 26th *Volksgrenadiers*, recalled to the Bastogne battle from their positions to the west by Hitler. The 35th Infantry Division, stretched out between Lutrebois and Harlange on the eastern shoulder of the salient, encountered tank and infantry units from 1st SS Panzer Division. The results were predictable. After heavy preliminary fighting, particularly in the east where two companies of 35th Infantry held out against wave after wave of determined German troops in the village of Villers-La-Bonne-Eau, the attacks bogged down. Neither side

RIGHT: *Some indication of the horrendous conditions that made operations so difficult in the latter stages of the battle. These tanks from the 3rd Armored Division have their 75mm guns sighted on the edge of a wood in case of ambush.*

achieved its objective – the Americans had not widened the corridor to any appreciable extent and the Germans had not cut it. The battle rapidly devolved into a slogging match, made worse by deteriorating weather conditions. At the same time, 26th Infantry Division made little headway in the hills and forests to the southwest of Wiltz, grinding to a halt around the small but important crossroads known as Café Schumann, dominated by the German-held Hill 490.

The pattern so painfully established on this day continued until well into the New Year, with anything up to 17 separate German attacks against Bastogne being experienced daily. Casualties were heavy on both sides and, inevitably, more and more units were drawn into the fray. On the American side 6th Armored Division reinforced the corridor on 30/31 December, followed a few days later by 17th Airborne, the third of the divisions belonging to Ridgway's XVIII Airborne Corps. Also in early January 90th Infantry Division joined the 26th around Hill 490 and the approaches to Wiltz. On the German side, as Manteuffel tried desperately to eliminate the salient – a process which reached even greater heights of ferocity on 3-4 January when he shifted his attacks away from the corridor to the

LEFT: *US engineers prepare to move tanks damaged in the fighting around Bastogne to the rear for repair work. The unit is the 9th Armored Division.*

RIGHT: *Tanks of the 7th Armored Division advance in support of infantry attacking high ground in the vicinity of St Vith, 25 January 1945.*

original defensive perimeter, still held by 101st Airborne – units from as many as eight different divisions were involved. Bastogne was in danger of becoming another Verdun.

The pattern was eventually broken by a number of apparently unconnected events, many miles apart. The first of these occurred just before midnight on 31 December, when Hitler's offensive against 6th Army Group began. Codenamed Operation *Nordwind*, this was an attempt to pinch out the Allied salient in the Vosges Mountains by a number of coordinated attacks from north and south. The plan was conceived in outline at much the same time as *Wacht am Rhein* but only recently put together in detail. Infantry and armored divisions were to punch through the overstretched American defenses west of the Vosges and along the north-south spine of the mountain chain itself, outflanking the US VI Corps and sealing the Severne gap. At the same time units of the Nineteenth Army were to break out northward from the Colmar Pocket to surround Strasbourg and complete the encirclement of the salient. On paper the idea was feasible and could act as a significant diversion, forcing the Allies to withdraw troops from the Ardennes and so release the pressure on Model's units. This, in turn, would enable the drive on Antwerp to continue, with all its expected results.

In reality, however, *Nordwind* never stood much chance of success and, far from breaking the Allied will to resist in the Ardennes, its subsequent failure undoubtedly demoralized Model's already tired and dispirited men. By 3 January the initial German assaults in the Vosges region had been blunted, partly by American defensive efforts and partly because the divisions allocated to *Nordwind* were not well equipped. Although fighting was to continue until the 20th, particularly between the Nineteenth Army in the Colmar Pocket and the French defenders of Strasbourg, the offensive was contained without upsetting the

Ardennes counterattack too dramatically. Eisenhower would probably have liked to use more of Devers' divisions around Bastogne, but when those divisions were inflicting considerable losses on the Germans in their own area, this was hardly a cause for major concern. What was more important to the Allies was that Hitler had committed the small reserve he had left in the West to a battle away from the Ardennes sector. Before the New Year was three days old it was apparent that the Bulge contained as many German units as it was ever likely to, at a time when American reinforcements were still pouring in.

It was not just the German ground forces that were dissipated in this way. On 1 January 1945 the Luftwaffe committed a similar strategic error. At 0745 hours more than 1100 fighters and fighter-bombers took off in four massive formations to attack American forward airfields. The aim was to destroy air opposition to a renewed land drive on Antwerp, but it was a forlorn and costly gesture. Although considerable damage was imposed – a number of airfields were unusable for a week and almost 300 American aircraft were destroyed on the ground – the losses inflicted upon the Luftwaffe in the process were crippling. By the end of the day over 100 German planes had been lost and perhaps twice the number severely damaged while, of far greater significance, experienced pilots had been killed. The losses were irreplaceable and from then until the end of hostilities five months later the Luftwaffe was no longer a force to be reckoned with.

Thus when Montgomery's counterattack on the northern flank of the Ardennes bulge began on 3 January, the odds had shifted decisively in favor of the Allied armies. Responsibility for the assault lay with Collins' VII Corps, comprising the four divisions originally assigned to him in December. They were concentrated to the east of the Ourthe River with 82nd Airborne protecting their left. British troops had been

RIGHT: *Another scene depicting the conditions faced by US troops during the attack on Herresbach.*

moved in to relieve 2nd Armored and 84th Infantry Divisions west of the river, and these two units joined 3rd Armored and 75th Infantry with the intention of driving down the Bastogne-Liège road from Manhay to Parker's Crossroads at Baraque de Fraiture, preparatory to a link up with Patton's forces at Houffalize. In the event 75th Infantry Division was kept in reserve and replaced in the frontline by the 83rd. Opposing them were 2nd SS Panzer and 12th and 560th *Volksgrenadier* Divisions, occupying defensive positions in rapidly deteriorating weather conditions.

The attack began at 0830 hours on the 3rd but because of icy roads and deep snow made little initial headway. By the end of the first day's fighting an advance of two miles only had been achieved and it was not until 7 January that units of 2nd Armored managed to take Baraque de Fraiture. This was sufficient to cause grave concern at OKW headquarters, where Hitler was at last forced to recognize the failure of *Wacht am Rhein*. In a series of meetings on 8-9 January he redeployed his forces accordingly. Fifth Panzer Army was ordered to withdraw to occupy a north-south line between Dochamps and Longchamps, west of the Bastogne-Liège road, and Sixth Panzer Army was pulled back to the east of St Vith and Wiltz, with II SS Panzer Corps (comprising the remnants of 1st, 2nd, 9th

RIGHT: *Weary US paratroopers trudge through a snow-covered track deep in the Ardennes.*

LEFT: *A GI contemplates the dangers of crossing the snow-covered expanse of an open field.*

BELOW LEFT: *General Eisenhower (left) congratulates General Patton for his central role in destroying the Ardennes pocket. General Omar Bradley, commander of the 12th Army Group, looks on.*

and 12th SS Panzer Divisions) being extracted entirely from the Ardennes sector for refitting as a future reserve. These moves took until 22 January to complete in conditions of chaos and continued fighting, but the fact that they were ordered at all marked the end of any remaining hopes for German success.

Thereafter the blows fell thick and fast upon Manteuffel's hard-pressed men. On 9 January Patton launched his counterstroke northward from the Bastogne salient with a total of eight divisions, 4th and 6th Armored, 26th, 35th, 87th and 90th Infantry and 17th and 101st Airborne. At first the emphasis was on the German pocket concentrated against the eastern shoulder of the corridor, west of Bras. For this a combined assault, delivered by 6th Armored and 35th Infantry from within the Bastogne perimeter and by 90th Infantry from the Café Schumann crossroads, was put into effect. The fighting was hard, particularly to the northwest of Café Schumann where 90th Infantry suffered heavy casualties. However, by 11 January the two arms of the pincer had linked up at Bras, trapping an estimated 15,000 enemy soldiers, most of them belonging to 5th Parachute Division, in a pocket which was rapidly cleared. At the same time 4th Armored and 101st Airborne began to move out of the Bastogne perimeter to the north, pushing toward Noville and Houffalize. News of a major Soviet offensive on the upper Vistula River, launched on 12 January, caused Hitler to transfer what remained of Sixth Panzer Army to the Eastern Front on the 14th, and this relieved the pressure significantly in the Ardennes. By 15 January the northern and southern arms of the Allied counteroffensive were within patrolling distance of each other and the link up was effected at Houffalize the following day.

As soon as this took place, Bradley resumed responsibility for Hodges' First Army and the subsequent mopping-up operations were a purely American affair. As the combined forces turned eastward to push the last of the German troops out of the Bulge, further counterattacks were launched from the original shoulders heading north from Echternach and south from Elsenborn. On 23 January, as the German retreat degenerated into a disorganized exodus, Brigadier General Clarke led CCB of 7th Armored Division back into St Vith and by the 28 January American soldiers stood once again along the lines they had occupied on 16 December. It had been a long, hard road to victory.

The Ardennes battle – the 'Battle of the Bulge' – cost the Americans over 75,000 men (8497 killed, 46,000 wounded and 21,000 missing or in German POW camps), but in the process they destroyed the cream of Hitler's remaining formations. German losses were nearly 120,000 (12,652 killed, 57,000 wounded and 50,000 captured), a loss rate which prevented the creation of any future reserve within the Reich to stand against the remorseless assault from both East and West. Thus, although *Wacht am Rhein* may have succeeded in delaying Allied advances by about six weeks, the battle left Germany poorly defended and vulnerable, characteristics which undoubtedly contributed to her early defeat. The 'master stroke' in the West had failed, the odds cut short by the stubbornness and courage of the American soldier.

APPENDIX

1. Units Involved, 16 December 1944-28 January 1945

A. Allied

(Organization, often extemporized, during the battle)

US First Army
 V Corps
  1st Infantry Division
  2nd Infantry Division
  9th Infantry Division
  99th Infantry Division
 VII Corps
  2nd Armored Division
  3rd Armored Division
  75th Infantry Division*
  84th Infantry Division
  (*75th replaced by 83rd Infantry
  Division from 3 January 1945)
 VIII Corps
  9th Armored Division
  14th Cavalry Group
   (from 2nd Infantry Division)

  28th Infantry Division
  106th Infantry Division
 XVIII Airborne Corps (created as
 reinforcement from reserve)
  7th Armored Division
   (from Ninth Army)
  30th Infantry Division
   (from Ninth Army)
  17th Airborne Division ⎱ (from
  82nd Airborne Division ⎰ SHAEF
  101st Airborne Division ⎰ reserve)

US Third Army
 III Corps
  4th Armored Division
  26th Infantry Division
  80th Infantry Division

 XII Corps
  10th Armored Division
  4th Infantry Division
  5th Infantry Division
 The following units were committed to the
 Bastogne salient in the final stages of the
 battle:
  6th Armored Division
  11th Armored Division
  35th Infantry Division
  87th Infantry Division
  90th Infantry Division
 Also involved:
  British XXX Corps (British Second
  Army 21st Army Group): 29th Armored
  Brigade

B. German

Sixth SS Panzer Army
 I SS Panzer Corps
  1st SS Panzer Division
  12th SS Panzer Division
  3rd Parachute Division
  12th *Volksgrenadier* Division
 II SS Panzer Corps (Reserve)
  2nd SS Panzer Division
  9th SS Panzer Division
 LXVII Corps
  246th *Volksgrenadier* Division
  277th *Volksgrenadier* Division
  326th *Volksgrenadier* Division

Fifth Panzer Army
 XLVII Panzer Corps
  2nd Panzer Division
  Panzer *Lehr* Division
  26th *Volksgrenadier* Division

 LVIII Panzer Corps
  116th Panzer Division
  560th *Volksgrenadier* Division
 LXVI Corps
  18th *Volksgrenadier* Division
  62nd *Volksgrenadier* Division
 Reserve
  9th Panzer Division
  15th Panzer Grenadier Division

Seventh Army
 LXXX Corps
  212th *Volksgrenadier* Division
  276th *Volksgrenadier* Division
 LXXXV Corps
  5th Parachute Division
  352nd *Volksgrenadier* Division
 Reserve
  79th Infantry Division

 OKW Reserve
  3rd Panzer Grenadier Division
  9th *Volksgrenadier* Division
  Führer Begleit Brigade
  Führer Grenadier Brigade

 Also involved (attached to Sixth Panzer
 Army)
 150th Panzer Brigade (Skorzeny's
 commandos)
 Von der Heydte's parachutists

2. Casualties 16 December-28 January 1945

A. American
 Killed: 8497
 Wounded: 46,000
 Missing: 21,000

B. German
 Killed: 12,652
 Wounded: 57,000
 Captured: 50,000

3. Chains of Command, 16 December 1944

A. Allied

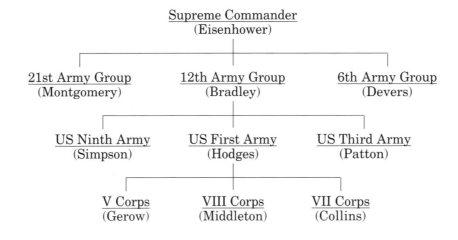

Supreme Commander
(Eisenhower)

21st Army Group   12th Army Group   6th Army Group
(Montgomery)   (Bradley)   (Devers)

US Ninth Army   US First Army   US Third Army
(Simpson)   (Hodges)   (Patton)

V Corps   VIII Corps   VII Corps
(Gerow)   (Middleton)   (Collins)

B. German

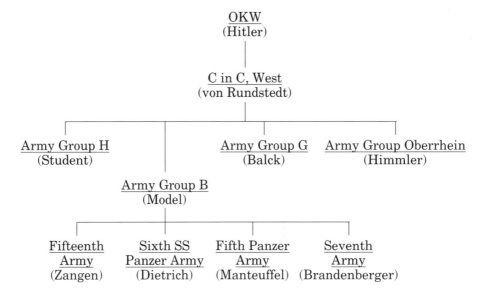

OKW
(Hitler)

C in C, West
(von Rundstedt)

Army Group H   Army Group G   Army Group Oberrhein
(Student)   (Balck)   (Himmler)

Army Group B
(Model)

Fifteenth   Sixth SS   Fifth Panzer   Seventh
Army   Panzer Army   Army   Army
(Zangen)   (Dietrich)   (Manteuffel)   (Brandenberger)

BELOW: *Generals Eisenhower and Montgomery confer over strategy.*

BELOW: *General Model, commander of Army Group B.*

INDEX

Page numbers in *italics* refer to illustrations.

ACKNOWLEDGMENTS

The author and publishers would like to thank Martin Bristow for designing this book and Moira Dykes for the picture research. The following agencies provided photographic material:

Bildarchiv Preussicher Kulturbesitz: pages 24, 28(top), 29(top), 41(top), 56(top).
Bison Picture Library: pages 2-3, 15(below), 16(below), 18(below), 19, 26(top), 41(below), 47(below), 50-51, 54(top), 55(top).
Bundesarchiv: pages 10(top), 12(top), 13(top), 15(top), 20(both), 25(top), 27(top), 32(below), 35(below), 45(below), 47(top), 60(below), 70(below), 71(both).
Hulton-Deutsch Collection: pages 8, 37(below), 46(below), 48, 55(below).
Imperial War Museum: pages 5, 9(below), 10(below), 11(below), 12(below),

13(below), 16(top), 17(below), 18(top), 21(top), 29(below), 30(both), 33(below), 34(below), 36(both), 37(top), 38-39, 42, 45(top), 54(below), 57(both), 58(top), 66(below), 68, 69(both), 73(top), 75(top), 76(top), 78(right).
Robert Hunt Picture Library: pages 25(below), 26(below), 27(below), 32(top), 33(top), 35(top), 40, 43(both), 44(both), 46(top), 49(both), 53(below), 56(below), 60(top), 64, 65(top), 66(top), 67(below), 70(top), 74, 75(below).
US Army: pages 14(below), 21(below), 22-23, 53(top), 59, 61(both), 67(top), 68(below), 72, 78(left)/**MARS:** 6-7, 31, 34(top), 58(below)/**TRH:** 9(top).
US Department of Defense/TRH: page 17(top).
US National Archives: pages 11(top), 14(top).
US Signal Corps: pages 62-63, 65(below), 73(below), 76(below).